Advance Praise for *The Frugal Editor*

Carolyn Howard-Johnson has done it again! Whether you're writing your first book or tenth, *The Frugal Editor* is a must-read.
~ **Tim Bete, director, Erma Bombeck Writers' Workshop and author of *In The Beginning . . . There Were No Diapers***

You'll want to keep handy Carolyn Howard-Johnson's practical guide to editing and refer to it every time you finish a piece of work, whether it be a query letter, a simple pitch, or a novel. Use her system step-by-step and you will very likely see your work change from an attractive lump of coal to a polished diamond editors won't be able to refuse.
~ **Magdalena Ball, editor of *The Compulsive Reader***

In this invaluable (and yes, accessible and engaging, too!) resource, Carolyn Howard-Johnson masterfully elevates an oft-misunderstood practice into the critical component of writing that it is. Don't turn in anything until you turn to this book.
~ **Peter Bowerman, author of *The Well-Fed Writer* series**

You hit the nail on the head with *The Frugal Editor*. You've pointed out the gremlins and simplified the eradication process. What more could a writer/editor/publisher ask for?
~ **Peggi Ridgway, author of *Successful Website Marketing* and other business books**

The Frugal Editor: Put Your Best Book Forward To Avoid Humiliation and Ensure Success will become a well-used reference for writers around the world.
~ **Cheryl Wright, editor of Writer2Writer**

Good editing is like honest business accounting: If you don't have it, you end up with a mess. *The Frugal Editor* is a must for the novice writer who needs to make that ideal first impression and the writer with a tenth book hitting the shelves who has become complacent about his brilliant prose.
~ **Kristin Johnson, author and writing consultant**

Most writers would never be so self-destructive as to submit an unedited manuscript for consideration, but agents and publishers tell us it happens often. To me, that's tantamount to showing up at a job interview wearing a T-shirt and flip-flops. So much success in life depends on actions the performance of which does not guarantee success, but nonperformance guarantees failure. Take it from editors and publishers: Never submit an unedited manuscript. I myself have a shelf of reference books on writing, grammar, style and editing. One of those is *The Frugal Editor: Put Your Best Book Forward to Avoid Humiliation and Ensure Success* by Carolyn Howard-Johnson.

~ Virgil Jose, writer and freelance editor

Nothing demonstrates professionalism like a well-edited submission. Follow Carolyn Howard-Johnson's clear, step-by-step self-editing approach for putting your *Best Book Forward* and you'll submit like a pro.

~ Gregory A. Kompes, conference coordinator of The Las Vegas Writer's Conference

The

Frugal Editor

Other Books by Carolyn Howard-Johnson

The Frugal Book Promoter: How to Do What Your Publisher Won't ~ USA Book News' Best Professional Book, 2004, and winner Book Publicists of Southern California's Irwin Award, 2006; published by Star Publish

This Is the Place ~ Eight awards, including Sime-Gen's Critics' Choice, 2001; published by AmErica House

Harkening: A Collection of Stories Remembered ~ Three awards, including Word Thunder's Excellence in Writing, 2002; published by AmErica House

Tracings ~ a chapbook of poetry named "Ten Best Reads of 2005" by the Compulsive Reader and received the Military Writers' Society of America's Award of Excellence; published by Finishing Line Press

Anthologies and Forewords: A Sampling

Forewords

Support Our Troops ~ By Eric Dinyer, foreword by Carolyn Howard-Johnson; published by Andrews-McMeel, 2005

Effort and Surrender ~ By Eric Dinyer, foreword by Carolyn Howard-Johnson; published by Andrews-McMeel, 2005

Anthologies

Pass Fail: 32 Stories about Teaching, from Inspiring to Hilarious ~ Edited by Professor Emeritus Rose A. O. Kleidon; published by Red Sky Press

Secrets: Fact or Fiction ~ Edited and compiled by Diane J. Newton; published by WingSpan Press, 2006

How To Do It Frugally Series

The Frugal Editor
Put Your Best Book Forward to Avoid Humiliation and Ensure Success

By
Carolyn Howard-Johnson

Red Engine Press
Branson, Missouri

Published by **Red Engine Press**

Library of Congress Cataloging-in-Publication Data

Howard-Johnson, Carolyn.
   The frugal editor : put your best book forward to avoid humiliation and ensure success / by Carolyn Howard-Johnson.
         p. cm.

ISBN 978-0-9785158-7-4
   1. Editing.   I. Title.
   PN162.H67 2007
   808'.027--dc22

                                                    2007015190

Cover by T. C. McMullen
Edited by Trudy McMurrin

Printed in the United States of America

Quantity discounts are available on bulk purchases of this book for educational institutions or social organizations. For information, please contact the publisher:

publisher@RedEnginePress.com

Dedicated to

my longtime critique partners, tough editors and writing-hearts,
JayCe Crawford and Leora Krygier
and to writers everywhere who are willing to admit
that as writers we cannot stand alone.

Why This Book Is Part of the
How To Do It Frugally Series

1. I know that no matter how I scold, there will be authors who will not hire an editor because they, too, are frugal or because they are so confident of their own skills they deem such a service unnecessary (a danger sign, by the way).

2. I know some authors will hire under-qualified editors and will be unable to discern the difference between an editor and a typo hunter. If—as you read this book—you come to this realization, you may need to start over with another, more capable editor.

3. After reviewing edits made on my books by fine editors, I learned that no matter how skilled an editor, the author needs to know a lot about the process, too.

4. I know that the cleaner the copy you hand over to your editor, the more accurate she can be. It may also cost you less in terms of her time and the money she charges you for that time.

The

art.– A word placed before nouns to limit or individualize their meaning.

Fru'gal

adj.– 1. Economical in the use or appropriation of resources; not wasteful or lavish; wise in the expenditure or application of force, materials, time, etc.; characterized by frugality.

2. Sparing; economical; saving, as, a frugal housekeeper; frugal of time.

Ed'i-tor

n.– 1. One who revises and prepares for publication.

2. One who directs the publication and policies of (as a news-paper).

Best

adj., superlative of good– 1. Excelling all others.

2. Most productive.

3. Largest, most.

Book

n.– 1. A collection of sheets of paper, or similar material, blank, written, or printed, bound together. Commonly, many folded and bound sheets containing continuous printing or writing.

2. A composition, written or printed; a treatise.

For'ward

adj.– 1. Being near or at or belonging to the front.

2. Eager, ready.

3. Brash, bold.

4. Notably advanced or developed; precocious.

5. Moving, tending, or leading toward a position in front.

6. Of, relating to, or getting ready for the future.

Acknowledgments

Inspiration comes from unexpected places. A few years ago, when I was interviewing for an instructor's position at the UCLA Extension Writers' Program, I mentioned that I was considering writing an e-book on book promotion, that all I'd learned from the School of Hard Knocks deserved to be passed on to unsuspecting authors. Linda Venis, the director of the Writers' and Literature Programs, loved the idea and thought that a course based on this idea was better than the one I had proposed. So, thank you, Linda. Thank you, UCLA.

But horrors. That interview was, perhaps, in February or March. I now had a class to teach that fall quarter and I could see how having a book on promotion would help my students. That wasn't enough time to query an agent, much less get a book published and released. Enter Kristie Leigh Maguire, an author I knew from the Web. She had been a publisher in one of her former lives, was starting a new company and said she could get a book out in plenty of time. She promised she could do both an e-book and a paperback before my deadline and pretty much twisted my arm to publish the paperback along with the e-book. Thank you, Kristie. Thank you, Star Publish.

That brings me to this book. Joyce Faulkner, author at Red Engine Press, asked me to write a couple of sections for the next book in her *The Complete Writer* series, one of them on editing. I thought if I was going to do that, I should propose a class to UCLA on that subject. I did. They accepted. I started to write. At the time I was doing a lot of editing and I kept getting ideas about elements that I should include in the *Complete Writer Publishes*. Soon I realized I had a book-in-the-making. Thank you, Joyce. Thank you, UCLA (again) and thanks to all you emerging and experienced authors whose typos and boo-boos gave me so many ideas for this book that a mere chapter would not cover them all.

Of course, I need to thank my editor, Trudy McMurrin (trudyedit@yahoo.com). Even authors who are darn good editors themselves need a different pair of eyes and a different skill set to edit their work, and if you don't think so, you really need this book.

I can't forget my other set of eyes, my husband Lance Johnson, author of *Everything Asians Need to Know About America, From A to Z*, published by Oriental Press in simplified Chinese. He has a great nose for typos. The two writers, supporters and friends who have been with me since before my first book was published, JayCe Crawford and Leora Krygier, are just plain instrumental in my writing life. Joyce Faulkner, author of *In the Shadow of Suribachi*, is also a chemical engineer and techno-genius. She is and will forever be my tech adviser. Others include Marilyn Ross, Magdalena Ball, Tim Bete, Peter Bowerman, Kathe Gogolewski, Peggi Ridgway, Kristin Johnson and Allyn Evans, all inspirations and experts known for helping authors in myriad ways. And the agents! Can't forget the literary agents who took their time to help me help you, including all of those listed in Appendix Four of this book.

I'd also like to thank the malicious gremlins, the *raisons d'être* for this book. They're the ones who put a damper on the publication of my first book, a novel called *This Is the Place*, and have continued to harass me to one degree or another ever since. Experience is the best teacher and now, I hope, my gremlin-slaying experiences will inform and inspire you.

CHJ

Contents

Gremlins, Horses, Writers and You

Why you — yes, you who aced English — need this book

Just as I was finishing this book, *Poets & Writers* published Peter Selfin's "Confessions of a Cranky Lit-Mag Editor." It was a kind of mini-rant on how authors influence editors negatively with minor (and not-so-minor) errors. He tells of one author who informs him in her cover letter that she has published three stories in the *New Yorker* and then "blunders into her essay with 'Growing up, there were two types of food in my family.'" He says it "reads like very sloppy editing" and goes on to reject the piece. (By the way, one of my readers with a master's degree could not identify the error here. If you can't, you will be able to by the time you've finished the section in this book where I talk about dangling participles. If you can't wait, use the index to find *dangling participles* to research this serious grammatical error now.)

The lesson here for all of us is that attention to detail and craft counts, and that even experienced writers can flub an opportunity if they don't pay attention to that last great step toward publishing, a good edit. Any author who had recently refreshed her understanding of participles by reading this book would not have dangled hers. At least, not that conspicuously.

Perfection is not possible. Even Editor Selfin admits he overlooks a mistake or two if the writer's voice captures his interest. With better editing we can guard against humiliation and in the process increase our chances for publication.

Carolyn Howard-Johnson

Leading a horse to water & other all-wet ideas about editing

In *The Frugal Book Promoter* I talk about branding. In that book, I felt a need to convince authors that *sales, marketing* and *promotion* are not dirty words, that we are participating in these disciplines every day when we brush our teeth and choose the proper clothing for whatever occasions loom on that day's calendar.

I don't need to convince most authors to be cautious about errors. There are so many writers who are so uptight about a typo creeping into their copy that their fear contributes to nightmares or at least to writer's block. Thus, *The Frugal Editor: Put Your Best Book Forward to Avoid Humiliation and Ensure Success* is an easy sell.

Where my job becomes difficult is in convincing writers that they need an editor—a real editor, an editor with credentials—before they begin to submit. Because I am also frugal, I recognize that my tendency to avoid spending money for something that will probably be done by someone else may well exist in other writers.

I know that many writers will nod their heads and then attempt the publishing process without an editor, even though they may have had the best intentions when they were agreeing with me.

I am also aware (because I hang out with writers of all kinds) that authors fear the sharp pencil point of an editor. These are usually new writers who are convinced that an editor will make their work into something other than what it is or will change it beyond recognition. I want to assure these writers that a good editor won't do that. A good editor will help a writer find her voice, remain true to it and still move the manuscript from a rough rock to a polished gemstone.

I agree that it is no fun to encounter unexpected flaws in one's book. If I hadn't, I wouldn't have written this one. However, mistakes in a writer's query letters, cover letters and book proposals can be more deadly than those in a manuscript. It is in these documents that editing failures can doom your entire book to failure. You and the quality of your book idea will be judged on these first contacts with agents, publishers, editors, and producers as surely as you would be judged at a board meeting if you left rats' nests in your hair that morning.

In this book I approach the editing process of every document as if it were a manuscript. It is easier to edit the much shorter introductions (queries, cover letters and proposals) that are being sent to the people who have the power to accept or reject your work, but the processes used are approximately the same. It is only a matter of degree between a full manuscript and your one-page query letter. So adapt the guidelines I give you accordingly. You, and only you, know where your strengths and weaknesses lie. You will know where to abbreviate or eliminate steps for these shorties, and for more intricate efforts (say, an academic thesis) you may want to expand on the processes I've suggested.

You probably already know that gremlins—very clever guys bent on chaos—are at work during the entire publishing process. You fight them with a vengeance, with every ounce of writing craft and publishing knowledge that exists in your body. If, however, a typo or grammar error slips through the careful net you cast for them, please don't lose any sleep. It will happen to every writer somewhere along her career path. Instead, be patient with yourself. And while you're at it, if you see an error in someone else's work, give the writer (and the publisher) the benefit of the doubt. It's all about Karma. We're all fighting the same gremlins here.

Many mistakenly use the word *editing* synonymously with finding typos. I worry that *The Frugal Editor* may contribute to that notion because it does not address essential elements of the writing craft like character development, setting or structure. Those are topics of their own. Reworking these aspects of writing really constitutes revision, not editing. Many complete books cover each of them thoroughly. For me to attempt to stipulate everything a polished manuscript needs would be impossible in one book. To cover revision topics briefly and then abandon the writer to struggle with incomplete understanding would not be in her or his best interest.

Carolyn Howard-Johnson

Therefore, I merely mention that your final draft should take these writing fundamentals into consideration because I can't assume that all authors will have undertaken revision before they move into editing. So, please, before you begin your editing process, review the larger elements of your craft. Experienced writers can approach this with the expectation that they may need only to fine-tune one or two elements of their books, but even minor learning curves are journeys worth taking.

You will see that I include some grammar guidelines here. You can tell these are not meant to be complete. I chose them because they are mistakes that many experienced writers (and editors) miss. I threw in a few of the ones that most writers understand but inadvertently make because when a writer does let them creep into her work, they are more noxious to my editing sensibility than the average error. I expect that when I mention some you already know, it will remind you not to backslide. It may even prompt you to check your references for more information on those subjects.

I want you to learn from this book just as I learned from writing it, but I'd also like you to enjoy the editing challenge, the process itself. Pretend the task before you is a puzzle. It's work. It's detail-oriented work. Still, it can be a lot of fun.

Have you ever run across a gremlin?

If he were only the guy in the Lamisil ad with purple warts on his head I wouldn't worry about him. You know, the one who causes toenails to yellow, the one you try to eradicate at the risk of executing your liver. According to the commercials, *that* gremlin is easy to avoid. Simply ask your doctor for Lamisil.

If you imagine the gremlin as the guy you had nightmares about when you were a kid, the one who hid under your bed and cleverly disappeared when your parents peeked under to search for him, well, he hasn't reappeared in decades. If he is the chap who showed up in fairy tales so we wouldn't get bored, we authors might welcome him as inspiration for a short story.

But no. He is the dirty, lowdown creep who will make the passive tense reappear in your manuscript after you've edited it twice, maybe three times. And he has relatives. Enough of them to plague every writer in existence. You won't be able to see them, won't know where they come from, but you'll know they have been at work when your book appears in print. Telltale signs will crop up in typos, grammar errors, widows, and other ugly formatting problems. So I worry about them a lot. You should, too.

I can't tell you how to eliminate these gremlins. After all, there are homicide laws. But I can tell you how to make their job harder. You recognize they exist and then purge any inclination you might have to let someone else bring them to justice. For as real as these gremlins are—regardless of how often we're told they're "only imaginary"—there is a myth that's passed on to us as truth. That's the story authors believe about editors and publishers.

We writers believe the stories because it's convenient to think that magical personages hired by publishers make books come off the press in immaculate form. Perfect. Pristine. That can happen, but I've come upon an occasional typo in books that are published by revered names in our industry. Worse, a few exist in my own books—more in some than in others. Some showed up before I knew I had to take charge of my own books' destinies. Some showed up after I knew that, but didn't know much about my part in editing. So, you can trust my hard-won experience when I tell you it behooves an author to do the very best she can—on her own —to eradicate the gremlins' work. If these guys get one up on Random House and Farrar, Straus & Giroux, other publishers and authors are easy touches.

So, how to do what seems to elude the best and brightest of word warriors? That's what I'm here for. I can't possibly cover all the possible tracks that gremlins leave, but I can pass along antidotes for what I see most frequently in the critique groups I facilitate and the classes I teach.

Some of this information will seem pretty basic, but you need to know the gremlin's secret. His motto is, "When authors and editors are looking for the big stuff, I'll diddle with the puny mistakes they're not likely to see." Of course, this guy is devious. He's not above going after more humiliating errors like using apostrophes in plurals. He knows your weak moments, your tired moments.

This book isn't only about what to watch for. It's also about how to make the editing process easier. You'll find lots of information; some that you will refer to time and again is in the sidebars. The sidebars are not listed in the table of contents. Mark them by creasing your page corners (you can tell I believe in making a book your own) or see your index under sidebars.

You'll also learn both manual and electronic techniques for digging errors out of your copy and keeping them out.

The most important part of the process is getting over the idea that someone else will do this for you or that it doesn't matter. It matters big. When you submit queries to agents. When you submit proposals to publishers. When your publisher submits a galley for you to examine and authorize. So bear with me. Make the guidelines in this book part of your working habits. You'll need several tricks up your own sleeve to keep all the gremlins at bay.

Section I
The Preliminaries

1 ༂ Misunderstanding Editing

The trouble with editing is that people misunderstand the word. Or they assign several meanings to it so that no one appears to fully understand what others are talking about. Further, the definitions of *editing, proofreading, galleys* and other publishing terms have changed drastically in the past decades as a result of innovations in the publishing industry, market upheavals and shifting responsibilities. Here is a mini-glossary so that as you and I work together, we'll be using a similar dictionary:

- **Revision** is not truly editing. It is reworking your piece and applies more to manuscripts than to short presentations like query and cover letters. It is the work you do between the first draft and the second, tenth or twentieth.

- **Editing**: This is what fine publishing houses used to do for all of their authors. They helped with the revision process and everything else until your manuscript was a butterfly in repose. No more. Leora Krygier, twice-published novelist, says, "Publishers do not want to edit anymore—they want to print a ninety-nine percent finished product directly from the author." It's a cost-cutting thing. Many publishers can't afford to give your book that attention they once did.

   If you want to be sure your precious book gets a full edit, you will hire an editor and you'll carefully check credentials when you do (I give you tips on how to do this in chapter twenty-nine—"Are You Convinced You Need an Editor?").

3

- **Line Editing**: This is what you'll get—if anything—from most publishers today whether they are on your publisher's staff or are independent contractors. The quality may be good or not. A line editor will catch some style problems, most grammar and, perhaps, ninety-nine percent of your typo and spelling errors.

- **Proofreading**: Proofreaders are typo hunters. Some might be insulted if you called them that, but that's what they are hired for, generally at low wages. Many "editors" you hire yourself (often without being careful about getting recommendations or about researching credentials) are capable of doing little more than typo hunting. Just the basics, Ma'am. Punctuation, spelling and typos, a modicum of grammar. The ones employed by publishers rather than by you may not be authorized to edit or rewrite, so they simply suffer in silence when they run across your dangling participles. Ditto when your dialogue tags need some work.

This book will help you with all of these processes except the revisions. Clearly, you will be practicing your editing skills—both the ones you already have and the ones you will learn from this book—from the first time you put fingers-to-keyboard. Your editing will go much more smoothly if you've thoroughly revised your manuscript first.

4

2 ≋ Organizing Only Feels Like Procrastination

Setting up your surroundings for the editing process is so much fun it may feel as if you're procrastinating. Relish the experience. Clear your desk of piles of stuff so tall you can't see over them, but don't be tempted to take on the tasks you find buried in them; they waited this long, they can wait longer. Put the papers, notebooks and clippings aside or file them and enjoy feeling naughty. When your environment is about as tidy as it will ever get, these essential steps come next:

- If you don't work with Word's **Spelling and Grammar Checker** all the time, set it up. (The computer-challenged will find instructions in the sidebar titled "Your Flawed Friend.")

- Make a place close by on your desk for *The Chicago Manual of Style* and your other spelling and reference books. (See the sidebar for your bare-essential recommended reading and references.) You should be able to reach them without moving your fanny from your chair.

- Stow similar online references somewhere in your computer where they can be easily accessed.

- To be certain that you don't pick up an old copy of your manuscript from your folder during the editing process, you:

  1. **Save** the copy of your manuscript with the title and a code to indicate it is original. Because I still don't quite trust computers (or electricity), I also run a hardcopy

5

and file it. Sometimes I e-mail a copy to my daughter for safekeeping on her Mac hard drive.

2.   Then click on **Save As** to make a new file. Use a new title —something like "ThisisthePlaceEdit1" or "FinalEdit."

3.   Label each and every page in your manuscript with this title by using the **header/footer function** in your Word program. That way, no matter where you are working within the manuscript—whether online or off-line—you will be assured that you are working in the correct copy of your manuscript. You'll also find that confirming (and soothing) information in the very top bar of your screen near the Word icon. The bar will be blue unless you've customized your screen colors.

Your Essential Desk References

- *The Chicago Manual of Style*
- *Associated Press Stylebook*
- *Elements of Style* by Strunk, White and Angell (Don't use one from 1950.)
- Your favorite thesaurus
- A good dictionary (Microsoft Word language functions are not a substitute.)
- Special vocabulary dictionaries for dialect, jargon, scientific or tech terms
- Rhyming dictionary
- *The Describer's Dictionary*

Need a guide to help you style computer terms? Go to:
www.geocities.com/ikind_babel/babel/babel.html

Those who are computer savvy will want to put important references for their work into their computer's **My Favorites** and add to it as they proceed with different tasks.

- During certain stages of your editing process, you'll want to turn on the **Track Function**—two clicks on **TRK** at the bottom of your screen. The colors may be changed by right-clicking on **TRK** and then on **Options** in the window that pops up. That way, if you work with an editor or ask for any other kind of input, that person's suggestions will be color-coded—a far more valuable feature than you can imagine until you need to discern one editor's input from another's. Later in this book (in Section III—"Let Your Computer Do What It Does Best") you'll find a sidebar on how to track.

- To keep the editing process from becoming daunting, tackle the manuscript with one kind of edit at a time. Start with a relatively easy project, or something creative to get you in the mood for the big job you are about to undertake. I like doing adverb searches because they allow me to think of this project as creative rather than drudgery. You'll find more on adverb search and seizure in chapter twelve —"Hunting Down Your Dreaded Adverbs."

- Schedule enough time to do individual editing projects at one sitting. Doing bits of jobs here and there plays into the hands of gremlins. In the long run, executing projects in one sitting saves time; you'll remember details instead of having to double check.

- Set your Word program for manuscripts. That means double spaced, margins exactly as Word fixes them for you, pages numbered on the right (if you install them on the left, they will not be visible when the pages are clipped). Don't save paper by printing on both sides. Don't flirt with fancy type faces for your titles. Don't even dare play with sans-serif. In my opinion sans-serif is elegant. Arial is an example. Still, research tells us that it is more difficult to read, most editors will be unimpressed by your effort and some will be downright annoyed. I submitted my first poetry book manuscript to an untold number of contests (and paid the fees) before I discovered that many contest readers would junk the entry without reading it as soon as they ran across even the poems' titles formatted in Arial. That affectation shouted, "Novice! No need to continue reading!" I think they missed some poems of pure genius but who am I (or you) to argue with a gatekeeper?

Your Flawed Friend

Word's **Spelling and Grammar Checker** is like a good friend. We come to understand it, accept its faults and love it for what it is.

To make it work for you, go to **Tools** on your menu bar, scroll down to **Options**. When the Options Window opens, choose the **Spelling and Grammar** tab and put a check in the box labeled **Spelling as you type**. In the section at the lower part of the window put a check in the box where it says **Check grammar as you type** and also where it says **Show readability statistics**. (We'll talk later about what that will do for you.) For now, be aware that after you've run a spelling and grammar check, a window will pop up that will let you discover details about your writing. Look at the other options to see if there is anything else there you think will be helpful to you. Be sure to click the **OK** button at the bottom of the window before closing it.

If you are interested in how **Flesch Readability** scores can help your writing, check Appendix Three (the Recommended Reading section) at the end of this book for an MP3 or CD-ROM audio on the subject offered by Double Dragon Publishing.

3 ≋ Best Book Forward: Your Editing Is Branding, Too

So what does editing have to do with your branding as an author? When we brand, everything counts. That includes the way you present yourself as you, the thoroughbred of the writing world, are coming out of the gate. You want your best colors showing.

Many of you reading this book have also read *The Frugal Book Promoter*, so you know about branding. Or you know how important branding is from your experience in the business world. Some of you may not have heard the word used this way. Branding is as important to writers as it is to General Motors or Swisher. If you don't know what Swisher is, then they haven't done a great job of branding—at least not to you. You do have a firm image of Coke. Now, those people know branding!

Your best colors include not only flawless (or as close to it as you can possibly come) editing but the way your edited material is presented. Shoot for *superior quality* by putting whatever you send out on good paper and a letterhead that fits well with how you want to be perceived as an author, including (if you wish) your own logo.

Your e-mail should also be professional. You should have an auto-signature for your e-mails (it's only thoughtful; editors don't want to be scrounging around for essential information). Know, too, how to write concise but interest-catching subject lines. As an example you'll want to use the term *Media Release* not *Press Release* and follow that with a phrase that will compel an editor to open his mail.

These niceties are related to editing, but they are also part of your marketing and branding. They are covered in the first book of the *How To Do It Frugally* series. Right now, however, as part of the branding aspect of putting your best book forward — your best self forward — order your stationery and explore your e-mail program for the **Signatures** function.

Section II
The Handiwork of Publishing

4 ❧ Digging In: Letting the Hardcopies Fly

Just about the time you believe you're ready to submit anything from a letter to a manuscript, that's when the real work starts. I've divided this book between the kinds of edits best done manually and those you can let your computer help you with—rather like letting your "fingers do the walking." The manual edits are more like letting your instincts and experience do the heavy lifting.

Every editorial or proofreading job should be done manually at least once. That is, every text you write—whether it is a full manuscript or a short query letter—deserves a manual edit before it sees an envelope or hears the click of the send button on your e-mail screen. That means you work from a printout—real paper, real ink, rested eyes that haven't been staring at screen glare all day. I prefer to edit twice or, as your doctor is fond of saying, "as often as needed." That way, when I begin to edit on-screen I have fewer errors to spot.

> **Save a Tree**
>
> Do a tree a favor. During the editing process, print out copies on paper you've recycled from other edits. To do this, put your salvaged reams into your printer tray clean side up. It will be your reward when you print out your final copy for submission on pristine paper, one side only.

Even though this is a hardcopy edit, not a new draft, I make every correction I see. Spelling. Grammar. Typos. Dialogue tags. If I notice major problems with structure, I go back to the computer to fix them immediately. We'll discuss formatting in more detail later but I don't believe in saving up corrections until the very last pass through a manuscript. This includes formatting tweaks, which are traditionally thought of as the job of the publisher. When galley time comes, you may well become the editor of your publisher's formatting boo-boos. You may as well make that job easier on yourself now.

I like to use labels to tag situations I'll need to work with later. I fold the label over the edge of the page and make a note on it, then take my time to write what changes I had in mind on that specific hardcopy page. I've been known to get sloppy and, when I do, several days hence I may not fully understand the edit I intended. That's another trick the gremlins use. I suspect they own wands that induce senile moments.

And, while we are talking nitty-gritty stuff here, a talented writing friend, Kathe Gogolewski, entered a contest that gave her feedback as part of the entry fee. She was surprised that she had been docked two points for not starting her short story manuscript one-third of the way down the first page. She says, "When you're getting close to the finalist stage [in a contest], a few points can make all the difference." If we think of the package we present to agents and publishers as a contest, the same concept applies. The margin between acceptance and rejection can pivot on font or first-page presentation.

5 ≈ Dangerous Corners Ahead: Covers and Queries

R eaders and editors, those who first learn about you in your cover letter, query letter, or proposal, know that when writers begin any one of these documents they tend to revert to copy full of business-ese. Some gatekeepers have a sense of humor about this and others are not so generous; you will learn later in chapter ten—"Let's Peek into the Minds and Query Boxes of Literary Agents"—what tests their patience.

Because your introductions to professionals in the industry are so important, these short documents should be edited first in hardcopy. Avoid excessive adjectives and self-assessments. In introductory documents *awesome* is a four-letter word. Wordiness, too. Ditch *literally* and *virtually* and anything else that sounds stiff or phony.

Stay away from words based in Latin with lots of syllables; it isn't only the long ones that can make you sound stiff. Your book is *titled*, not *entitled*; you *live* somewhere, not *reside*. You *buy* a book when you're talking to your neighbor. Why suddenly flaunt *purchase*? In a TV interview, Meg Ryan was asked what word she loved. She screwed up her face as only she knows how and turned the question around. She said she hated the word *enjoy*. "What's wrong with *liked* or *loved*?" she said. Who would have guessed? We can't avoid everything that makes every editor (or actor) peevish, but we can try.

The whole publishing world dislikes the term *fictional novel*. Novels, by definition, are fiction. A lead sentence that says, "I am hoping you will take a look at my fictional novel" is a dull lead, so that makes two strikes against you in one sentence. (Actually three. You don't need *am* or that *ing* — more about that later, too.)

We are often told not to be apologetic or self-deprecatory in cover or query letters and, of course, that is true. Avoid saying "I think" or "I believe." Just state the facts. Occasions when an apology may be in order are rare. The sample cover letter in Appendix Five of this book gives you an idea of when one might be appropriate. Certainly, never apologize for your book or your credentials.

There is another arcane rule — much ignored — that so narrowly affects our language it is rarely an issue. It does affect authors who work with titles. Let's take *The New York Times*. That's their title and it includes the *The*. So if you were a staff writer reporting on the stylistic independence of that paper, how would you write the lead for your article?

New York — Wednesday the *The New York Times* decided to go against practically every stylebook in existence and use *Web site* rather than *website* within their hallowed pages.

Well, hardly. You wouldn't use two of the word *the* in a row.

You will encounter this problem often if the title of your book starts with *the*.

This is an obscure consideration and therefore grammarians don't hold forth on the subject often. *The Chicago Manual of Style* says, "A *the* preceding a name, even when part of the official title, is lowercased in running text." That means if your book is titled *The Longest Day of the Year*, you'll often need to lowercase that initial *T*, and you won't italicize it. The easiest way to solve this problem is to avoid constructions that force you to address it. The great Chicago stylebook doesn't tackle the problem if the title is the first part of a sentence because, after all, *The* will be capped by virtue of being the first word in that sentence. Aah, saved by the easiest grammar rule in any book! But then you'll have to decide whether or not to keep *the* italicized (because it is part of a title). If you follow the guideline above to its logical conclusion, you won't, but I couldn't find a source that would even touch that one.

Whew! So why did I title my book *The Frugal Book Promoter*? Pure ignorance. And why did I stick with a similar title for this book? It's all about branding, something I discuss in more depth in that book on promotion. Besides, now that I know the style guideline, it's easier for me than it was.

6 ≋ Let's Make Everyone Agree

An important manual edit is one that checks to see if plural pronouns match their singular antecedents and vice versa. Recently I co-edited *The Complete Writer's Journal* for Red Engine Press. Experienced and emerging authors, promoters and publishers were invited to submit quotations for this journal. It was to include more than one hundred and serve not only as a gift item or practical tool for writers, journalers or sketchers, but also to be an effort in cross promotion.

In these submissions, I found dozens of these seemingly innocuous agreement errors. Some of these entries were so good that my fellow editors and I wanted to use them anyway; we decided to wield our editorial powers to fix them. We sent the edits back to the authors for final approval and I'll be darned if several didn't send their quotations back to us in their original form. My point is that these mismatches are so shifty we don't notice them or we make excuses for them.

Here's an example of a submission we didn't accept: "E-books can be a great promotional tool." Arguably, the author may have thought of *e-books* as a collective term for electronic publishing (and therefore singular). Still it would have been easy to eliminate the ambiguity by making it: "E-books can be great promotional tools" or "E-book technology can be used as a great promotional tool." Of course, you have to identify these errors or ambiguities before you can edit them.

The pronoun/antecedent error is a likely invitation for a professional to judge the writer an amateur. The gremlin knows this; he also knows that in longer sentences they are difficult to spot. They'll often slip by several readers, and that makes him a very happy gremlin indeed.

While you're looking for singular and plural anything, make sure your verbs agree with the true subjects of your sentences, for these mismatched pairs are also the gremlins' lurking instruments.

7 ⚏ Cut-and-Paste Errors: The Way to a Gremlin's Heart

You are sure to use cut-and-paste when you edit. This process often leaves behind little telltale letters or words like *be, in, a* – literally hundreds of possibilities. They are meat and potatoes for gremlins and they thrive every time you make a major change in your copy. The worst are the ones that are real words so your spelling checker will not find them and often your grammar checker doesn't notice them either. They will hang in your copy indefinitely until reamed out by a careful reader. Someone – perhaps a friend who is as detail-oriented as an accountant or – this will become repetitious, I know – a very sharp-eyed editor. Your earlier writing patterns are part of your subconscious, so you almost certainly will miss at least some of these tiny guys in your own writing.

While you are scouring these leftovers from the cut-and-paste efforts in your last draft, look at your sentences that begin with conjunctions like *but, and,* and *so.* Yes, the grammar gurus say you can use these words to begin a sentence, but what if the gatekeeper who gets to vote "Yea" or "Nay" on your precious manuscript doesn't know what you know? You get to choose, but I wouldn't stake my credibility on any one of those words early in the acceptance game.

Titles Are Tattletales

Your expertise as a writer may be judged by how you punctuate your titles in any document you tuck into an envelope and send on its way:

- A work shorter than a three-act play or a complete book takes quotation marks. This includes short stories, essays, songs, poems (other than epics), and one-act plays. It also includes individual chapters from books, articles in periodicals including daily newspapers, and episodes or parts of serials on radio or television.

- Underline or italicize titles of larger works made up of smaller segments, including books, three-act plays, movies, the names of newspapers, magazines or journals, and the names of entire television or radio series. Movie titles, too, are underlined or italicized. Because the Internet underlines links, editors now may prefer italics for titles so they won't be mistaken for links.

- Legal documents, the Bible, the Qu'ran, the Torah, and other sacred texts do not take quotation marks, underlining or italics.

- Here are the general rules for capitalizing titles: First and last words are capped. So are all other words but the articles (a, an, the), conjunctions and prepositions of four or fewer letters. Much disagreement swirls around capping subtitles. The Brits prefer to cap only the first word in a subtitle.

Learn more about it at
www.ise.ac.uk/resourceswebEditorsHandbook/bestPracticeGuide
/editorailwriting/editorialWebStyleGuide.htm#Publication-titles

22

8 ≈ Getting Cute with Caps

Words typed all in caps are being used more and more on the Web. Sometimes they are meant to draw attention to a book's title. Sometimes to indicate that the writer is yelling. Sometimes to show that a word should be emphasized. Their use may become a habit you'll want to avoid in more formal presentations. They can be spotted easily during your first visual edit. See the "Tattletales" sidebar for rules governing titles.

9 ∿ Effusive Italics

Now that so many books are self- and subsidy-published, many have been put together by marginally qualified editors—or none at all. It has become common practice to italicize a character's internal dialogue. This is unnecessary. You will be writing from a specific point of view and your reader will be aware of what that POV is. You want to develop your craft, to trust your skills as a writer and your readers' ability to read well. Typography should not be part of this equation.

Using italics for internal dialogue in a document that introduces your craft to those who are the gatekeepers of your acceptance or rejection will indicate to them that you are not an experienced writer. Those first three chapters are important. Don't give your reader something to criticize unnecessarily. If your manuscript should be accepted in spite of this affectation and you are assigned a good editor, know that you will be expected to edit all those italics out before press time.

After you become familiar with using the Find Function for editing (more about this in Section III—"Let Your Computer Do What It Does Best"), you will see why corrections of this type are more quickly made during your first manual edit.

10 ≋ Let's Peek into the Minds and Query Boxes of Literary Agents

S peaking of not tipping an editor or agent off that you may not (yet) be a professional (or accidentally leading one to believe you aren't when you are), some of those professionals have been generous enough to help me help you avoid the mistakes they see most often. In fact, I was overwhelmed by the number of agents willing to take time to do this. Even many who didn't care to be mentioned responded with ideas for you.

I mention the names of those agents who have given me permission to use them here. If you choose to query any of them, please pay special attention to the first (Megan Atwood's) suggestion on the list below. In my unofficial survey it was the most mentioned breach of protocol in a search for a literary agent.

> **Tips from the Agent's Mouth?**
>
> Here is a blog from the mouth and heart of an agent. It will help you avoid the kinds of errors that turn agents off:
> http://pubrants.blogspot.com/

You will find these agents' names with contact information listed in Appendix Four. To tailor your query appropriately, you'll need to do your own homework by visiting their websites so you can respect their individual guidelines.

Megan C. Atwood, Firebrand Literary Agency: Like most agents, Megan wants queries only for the genres she sells. She also is not keen on blanket submissions and queries that are not personalized.

Megan also cautions against the "overuse of adjectives . . . a warning sign to me that this person is not a strong writer." She also advises against submitting a manuscript similar to one you submitted to her earlier—and she declined. Apparently agents have longer memories than writers credit them with.

Lisa Ekus-Saffer of **Lisa Ekus Public Relations Co. LLC** wants to know why you are the one to write this book. She also says she expects typewritten queries and says, "I kid you not!" Imagine how hard it would be for an agent if everyone submitted hand-written queries.

Lilly Ghahremani of Full Circle Literary LLC says that it's a turn-off when an author presumes too much. She says, "Just like you may not want someone on a first date to say, 'when we have our kids . . .,' it's uncomfortable for an agent to hear someone say, 'I can't wait for you to represent my book'!"

Scott Eagan, Greyhaus Literary Agency, says "You get one chance to pitch to me. If I pass on the story, trying to get me to change my mind will never work."

Matt Wagner, Fresh Books Literary Agency, offers up an example subsidy- or self-published authors should avoid as if their publishing careers depended on it (which they may). One of his queries said, "I self-published my book at Lulu. I haven't marketed it at all yet." His reaction? "Oh, okay, you mean that a previous round of agents passed on your project, which you then haphazardly published, and now you're too lazy to market your book but you think maybe someone else will take it over for you?"

He also cautions against sending him a novel that is only twenty thousand words. He says, "Uh, you mean a two-chapter book? Sorry, that's not long enough to be a book."

Michael Larsen of **Michael Larsen–Elizabeth Pomada Literary Agents** suggests authors follow through. He says, "Find out when you should expect to hear from agents and call or write them if you don't." He suggests authors disclose the fact when they submit to more than one agent at a time.

Kae Tienstra, KT Public Relations & Literary Services: Kae would like you to get to the point and don't get fancy on her. She points out that getting cute takes forever for a computer to load and doesn't much impress in real-time either. That is seconded by many, including **Liz Trupin-Pulli** of **Jet Literary Agency**. To ignore the suggestion because you feel being clever will make you stand out will be an effort in futility.

Kae also says that agents can tell when they're being "buttered up." She says, "We know you're impressed with our 'wonderful publishing credentials and vast experience' as agents. But, ya know? We've only been agents for a short time, so who are we kidding here?" Her comment is also a reminder to do that homework before you write your query.

Elaine P. English, PLLC Literary, says, "My biggest pet peeve is the author who describes his/her work as a 'fictional novel.'" She also will not read a cover, query or manuscript in anything less than a ten-point font (and many agents are not that generous). Twelve point is standard.

Stephanie Kip Rostan, Agent of **Levine/Greenberg Literary Agency, Inc.,** reminds authors not to query "every single agent at our agency." Either use a general submission form when it is provided or choose one agent whose biography is a good match for your project.

She also says, don't "slavishly follow a query letter template . . . . If you can't write a query letter on your own, I have to be concerned about your ability to write a book. Besides, it's just creepy."

Roberta Brown, Brown Literary Agency, cautions against comparing your work to that of another author. She says, "The bestselling author is already published, with a following. No editor wants a copycat."

Jenny Bent, Trident Media Group, reminds authors not to send a disk rather than a manuscript unless the agent specifically suggests it. She also warns against authors sending random chapters when she requested the first three consecutive chapters.

Jeff Kleinman of **Folio Literary Management** suggests that:

- It is presumptuous for authors to ask agents for feedback. He acknowledges they may get some from agents, but not to ask.

- Authors avoid promising an instant bestseller.

- An author's ability to pitch his book well has "more to do with [the author's] knowing the project is ready to go" than it does with selling it.

- An author should avoid appearing argumentative in the query letter.

Here are two to warm your heart: **Laurie Abkemeier** of **DeFiore and Company** says, "If I can't spot the diamond despite the soot, I'm the one who is making the fatal mistake." **Tamela Hancock Murray** of **Hartline Literary Agency** says that after careful consideration she can't "think of anything concrete that will cause me to reject a manuscript that has merit."

Michelle Wolfson of **Artists and Artisans Inc.** wants you to avoid trying to sell her more than one book in any given query letter. That's like bringing on a blind date "your three best friends and any brothers you may have in case I like one of them better." She wants you to choose your best and sell it with everything you've got.

Kristin Nelson of **Nelson Literary Agency LLC** warns against queries that are boring, too general, or inappropriate. She wants a good sum-up of the plot and a unique hook. Some agents are patient, though. She says if a query is formatted improperly, she may request that an author polish it and send it again so she can give it "a fair look."

Here are some suggestions from agents who prefer not to be identified:

- Don't start a query with a question.

- Who you are as a writer impresses some far more than a run-down on the "twists and turns of your book."

- Don't cold-call. Most of the agents I contacted prefer to be "warmed up with a query" letter. Some prefer no calls. Ever.

- Don't use mass e-mail submission services unless the service will tailor each query to the individual agent. So, if you use one, the person you hire to do it should be professional and leave no clues that the person submitting isn't you. Yes, I know some agents will hate that I said that but some authors do have day jobs, families and the next book to write.

What advice do agents have on manuscripts per se?

Gina Panettieri of **Talcott Notch Literary** reminds us that:

- Authors should not overuse sentence fragments as a style element.

- Authors who "overuse exclamation points . . . make their books sound as if they were written by a yappy Chihuahua on speed."

- A "lack of complete page headers on a manuscript can be a disaster for an agent" who may be working with a dozen manuscripts or more at one time.

- A "manuscript that lacks proper indentations for paragraphs is often too frustrating to read."

31

Jenoyne Adams, associate agent for **Levine/Greenberg Literary Agency, Inc.,** emphasizes doing a complete rewrite when it is suggested. Patching up a book in "less than three days almost always demands a rejection." She also likes an author to make sure the manuscript really begins long before page fifty. She says, "Save the back story for your research notebook."

Last but not least, I loved that **Larry Kirshbaum** of **LJK Literary Management** gave me another reason (without prompting!) to encourage you to read the first book in this series, *The Frugal Book Promoter*. He said, ". . . the author must have some important biographical items that can lead to publicity and promotion."

This is a partial list. It is a list sent to you from the hearts of agents who care. Enough said, except for one piece of advice from **Megan Atwood** not to take a rejection personally: "There have been several manuscripts I've had to pass on . . . but I loved them. That is always heartbreaking." As I read her comment, I thought it was a plea not to give up. Keep submitting but also keep improving your craft.

As authors, we need to understand more about agenting (and publishing). We need to work up a little compassion. Agents have businesses to run. They know who their contacts are, which books are likely to sell to those contacts. Only the agent knows his or her own track record, knows his or her other clients, can see how your book fits into his or her mix. If you've written well and done your homework, you will find an agent you click with.

Having said all this, I am now going to tell you something many agents will hate (but also understand). You may ignore the submission guidelines that require you to submit exclusively, at least at first contact. That goes for submission to agents, publishers, review journals and others. I know because when I was first getting started as a professional writer, I attended a conference called Summer Literary Semesters in St. Petersburg, Russia. On one of the panels sat editors from some of the most prestigious literary journals in the US. One of them said, "Ignore that rule. Even though we know it is to our advantage, we all also know it is patently unfair to authors." Those may not be his exact words; his exact words may have been considerably stronger. The other panelists all laughed and nodded. I didn't laugh. I applauded. Some of us could die of natural causes waiting for tandem readings.

If you decide to submit your manuscript to several publishers or agents at once, include that information in the cover or query letter. If you are uncomfortable with that, at the very least, track your submissions and let the unlucky (or slower) editors know when another elects to publish your piece. We authors can refuse to participate in something that does not benefit us in any way but we should still be as considerate as possible.

Section III
Let Your Computer Do What It Does Best

11 ≈ Use Word's Tools. Don't Trust Them

M any editors and writing teachers warn authors against using Microsoft Word tools for editing. That is understandable. They see writers let tools usurp craft. They see how the problems tools cause the unwary can outweigh their usefulness. Dr. Bob Rich, an editor, advises people to "just turn them off." (http://bobswriting.com/editing.html)

Though I don't consider myself a tekkie in any way, I use these dreaded tools because they can be time savers. You may already know how to make them work for you or feel it is valuable to learn. Over the years I published books in almost every way imaginable and during this painful (and joyful) process, I learned some tool-tricks for avoiding gaffes that leave smiles on the gremlins' faces.

Consider the source: Track every editor's suggestions

I believe in tracking corrections and changes. That's because any critique partner—a professional or someone who agrees to play the part of your typical reader—can be valuable in assessing your work. The thing is, each is valuable in a different way. As you edit, you'll want to know the source of a criticism so you can evaluate whether or not you want to accept a particular piece of advice. That's as important in the editing process as it is in a critique group setting where the way you choose to utilize advice depends on the source and expertise of the one providing the critique.

Because my handwriting is lousy and because tracking makes it easy for the author to accept or reject edits, I use it whether I am editing for myself or for someone else. Click. Click. It's in or it's out! If you hire an editor who works electronically, you may ask him or her to do the same for you.

Track Edits and Ideas

See the little button that says **TRK**? It's usually found near the bottom of your document, right above the bar that lists your open files. When you click it, Word will use colored font and colored edit balloons to tell you what is new, what is deleted, even what kind of formatting changes you make. This color can be changed with a right-click on the TRK button so you can color-code the input from each editor; that way you'll know who made a suggestion and can judge its reliability accordingly. When you use TRK, you can see the original copy right next to the edited copy and decide whether to accept or reject with a right-click and a tap on your mouse.

Note: The toolbar on which you find TRK must be active. If it is not, go to **Tools**, then to **Track Changes** to activate it. Your document must also be in the **Unprotected** mode as set from the **Tools** drop-down menu.

I also use **TRK**:

- To edit my own material when I want to know later what is new and what is old.

- When I have an idea I may want to insert but have yet to rate its brilliance quotient.

- So I can trace whom to credit for quotations or suggestions.

- When I reassemble or edit a second or revised edition of a how-to or textbook so I can distinguish new copy from old.

- To help me ascertain whether new information I add repeats what was in the work before. (I address other ways to determine if you've been repetitive later in this section. Also see the "Editing Elixir" sidebar for a computer program that will help with edits of this sort.)

Word's uncritical, undiscerning but thorough editing tool

Once you have finished your manual edits and are back to working on your computer, you can make corrections as you would when you write. You can also use the powerful gremlin fighter in Word, the **Find Function**. Do use caution because if you get swept away with FF's magical properties, the gremlins will appropriate it, and you may end up with more problems than you had when you started. So, keep it simple, start slowly and don't get fast and furious with the **Replace All** button.

The ABCs of Find Function

The easiest and most disaster-proof way to use your **Find Function**:

- Click **Edit** on your toolbar, then **Find and Replace.** The window that pops up will be set to the **Find** tab. Do not change it.

- Type in whatever you are trying to find. To avoid finding words you don't want to change, use spaces to isolate the computer's search. Example: to find the word *is* type: (space)*is*(space). That will keep your detail-oriented program from picking up the letters *i* and *s* in every word where they appear, such as *list*.

- In the **Find and Replace** window, click on the **Find Next** button to examine one occurrence at a time. Consider each one. Do not rush.

Among other things, your **Find** button can:

- Help find repetitive words and phrases. Use Word's **Thesaurus** to help you add variety, even to find a more precise word than your first choice.

- Individualize a specific character's speech pattern by intentionally using repetitive words (very subtly, please!) or grammar-specific constructions. (See chapter twenty

—"Enhance Your Characterization and Dialogue" for more on this subject.)

- Find overblown, redundant and overused adjectives.
- Find ineffective adverbs.
- Strengthen verbs.
- Identify passive tenses and eliminate them when appropriate. (We'll cover how you can use Readability scores available in Word to help you with this editing process later.)
- Rename a character or place.

Once you are proficient you may think of new uses on your own.

An Editing Elixir for the Computer Savvy

Concordance is a computer program that helps you analyze your documents with a plan you devise to suit your needs.
See: www.dundee.ac.uk/english/wics/wics.htm.

Joyce Faulkner, co-editor of *The Complete Writer*, says "it is a program that will find words that are used frequently so you can determine if they're used too often. You can do this manually, of course, but this is more accurate and a time-saver." A valuable tool for editors and self- and subsidy-publishers who are computer-savvy enough to tackle a new program, it can do much to refine the editing process, including:

- Make indexes and word lists.
- Count word frequencies.
- Compare different usages of a word.
- Analyze keywords.
- Find phrases and idioms.
- Publish to the Web.

12 ≈ Hunting Down Your Dreaded Adverbs

You may recall I mentioned that I like to begin the editing process by dredging up adverbs. You may have wondered why in the world-of-writing I would want to search for adverbs, which we all know are perfectly good parts of speech used frequently by the most scholarly among us.

They're ugly, that's why. They're often redundant. They cloak weak verbs. In fact, they are probably first cousins to the gremlin you want to remove. The good news: You can use your **Find Function** to root them out.

First, let's look for the obvious adverbs, words that end with *ly*. Type in *ly*(space). That space will keep Word focused on what you want to look at. Once each *ly* adverb is found, ask yourself:

Is this adverb redundant?

For example, "She ran quickly toward the car." The word "run" implies "quickly." Some of the adverbs you find won't be that blatantly repetitious, but if you concentrate on them, you'll see that many adverbs contribute nothing to what would be left if you axed them. You may feel that *quickly* is needed. Perhaps you're making a stronger point than the word *run* achieves on its own. Then consider the verb itself. It may be so weak it requires the adverb. By changing to a stronger verb, you strengthen the sentence and eliminate the adverb in one edit. If no appropriate substitute for that verb comes to you, use the **Thesaurus** that Word provides for

41

you. If you still are at a loss, use the real live one in that mini-library you prepared for the top of your desk. Consider *sped, rushed* or *sprinted*. We'll talk about other ways to replace adverbs with more original language in a bit.

Is this adverb related to *y'know*?

By that I mean, is this an adverb you stick into your copy for no other reason than it mimics the way you think or talk? Well, y'know, I really hate that and an agent or editor is going to . . . y'know . . . hate it even worse. Even if these words are part of a dialogue, you'll want to use them sparingly. More than a hint of an annoying verbal trait can easily tire your readers.

Your *ly* search may bring up many words in the *y'know* category *really* frequently. So, do you *really* need it? If you're a fiction writer and *really* is part of the speech pattern of your fourteen-year-old Valley Girl, you may want to spot a *really* here and there but do trim them somewhat so they don't become so annoying they take your reader out of the story. If not, and there is no other *real* . . . oh, no! good reason for keeping them—and be honest with yourself—purge them. Consider each—one by one—and be tough.

Is this adverb humiliating you and making your verbs look silly?

We've all seen those lists—often humorous—where adverbs split infinitives or where they modify the wrong word, idea or phrase. It is a good idea to go back over your entire document to assess adverbial placement after you've cleansed your manuscript of all the adverbs you can. It will be easier to spot misplaced adverbs when you can concentrate on this single problem. Use the general rule in the sidebar to assess the position of each adverb in a sentence.

> **Adverbs Are Fodder for Gremlins**
>
> Adverbs can occupy different positions in a sentence. The normal position of most adverbs is between the subject and the verb. The adverb normally follows the verb *to be.*

To find examples of how improperly placed adverbs can affect meaning, refer to your old desktop standby *The Elements of Style* by William Strunk Jr., E. B. White and Roger Angell. If your copy has been on your desk as long as mine has, consider buying an updated (fourth) edition to get the latest information. Our language is always changing but television geared those changes up and the Net has reset them to warp speed.

Here is a list of words that may serve as adverbs. Do an individual search on each one with an eye to your own habits. After a while you'll know your own writing routines well enough to narrow the searches to the most likely trouble causers. I starred those I find used incorrectly or overused most frequently in the editing I do.

almost	always	even *	far	fast
less	maybe	more	never	not
often *	only *	perhaps	really *	sometimes
seldom	soon	then	today	tomorrow
too *	usually	very *	well	yesterday

Editing your adverbs is like mining metaphor gold

Writers who want to liven up their copy can edit adverbs so they produce metaphors. (Remember the *Reader's Digest* feature "Toward More Picturesque Speech"?) Once when I was speaking to the Small Publishers of North America (SPAN), someone in the audience asked if there was a site that would give him a list of good metaphors to improve the imagery in his writing. I told him that if there was, it would probably be a list of clichés or a list of what would fast become clichés once everyone started using them. That was before I knew this adverb trick which works better than any list.

Your search for adverbs can yield metaphors or similes, the kinds of associations that allow you to find and insert flecks of solid gold into your copy. In the example we used before, "She ran quickly," you determine that the adverb is redundant. Running, by its nature, is quick. But you still want more than *quick*. Ask yourself, "quickly as what?" This kind of edit can open doors for better imagery—help give your reader a visual or other sensory experience. It can also suggest possibilities for humor—something that may be welcomed by agents or publishers skimming query letters or dull proposals.

One of the advantages of editing adverbs—indeed any kind of systematic editing—is that you'll begin to write more concisely. When you do, the gremlins may spot a professional and move to greener fields.

13 ≈ Death to Gerunds, Participles and Other Ugly *Ings*

Wait! I know your eyes began to look as if they were afflicted with inoperable cataracts at the very mention of these grammatical terms. Nevertheless, you may need this information even if you think you already know what these monikers mean. So bear with me and I'll make it painless.

We can use the **Find Function** to help eliminate unattractive gerunds and participles. (I know you can't wait for me to refresh your memory on these terms. Be patient. It's coming!) Though not all gerunds and participles are ugly, they do tend to slow down our copy and make it wordy. They coax us to use longer, less readable sentences. They get us into dangling participle trouble. Gremlins adore them. They may be difficult even for expert editors to identify because many are ingrained into our speech patterns. You'd better be prepared to eradicate them yourself.

We often hear the term *dangling participle*. It has a near-poetic ring to it. Trouble is, it's sometimes apparent that the person who uses the term doesn't know what one is. That may not indicate an earth-trembling gap in knowledge for us writers as long as we know how to avoid them. We'll need the grammar, though, to discuss how to shun them with any understanding. So here goes.

A participle is *part* of a verb, usually the part with an *ed*, an *ing* or rarely an *en* hanging off the end of it. These endings identify the verb as a participle. They're attached to the verb that comes after what we used to call *helper verbs* when we were in grade school. You know, the *haves* and *hases* that help give verbs their tenses.

However, dangling participles are not called *dangling* because they are the parts that come at the ends of multi-part verbs or because of those endings dangling from their roots. They're called *dangling* because writers use them to modify something other than what the writer intended.

"Tired of reading copy with dangling modifiers, the galley went soaring across the office right into the round file." You may know what the author intended here, but we all know that galleys can't read; thus this sentence illustrates a dangling modifier. That is, when we examine the structure, the meaning is illogical.

These dangling guys are sneaky to edit because the author knows what she is trying to say and doesn't pick up on the error (or the humor it creates). That's only one of the reasons that it's best to get an editor, even if she does have a short temper and sends galleys soaring across the room.

Not to worry. You're probably paying her. She'll retrieve it and rework the sentence that you didn't. This is not a flick-of-the-pencil edit, but she'll probably never let you know how your danglers tried her patience. But then your agent or publisher will never know about them either. That's a relief, no?

So, ignore that this edit involves scary grammar words and set the **Find Function** in your Word program to *ing*(space) (yes, use the **Spacebar** to keep the FF focused on *ings* at the ends of words rather than the ones hanging about in the middle of words). Examine each one.

Gerund *ings* can keep you from laughing all the way to the bank

Your **Find Function** almost certainly will pick up at least one inappropriate *ing* in your query letter. Probably in a sentence like,

"Writing is something I always wanted to do." *Writing* is a gerund. The magic of the English language lets us change the verb *write* into a noun by adding *ing* so we can use it as the subject of that sentence. Unfortunately, it also makes the sentence wordy and not very direct. Won't "I always wanted to write" do? Or actually improve it? That's how you analyze each of your *ing* finds.

While we're on the subject, you can probably find something more pertinent and original to tell an agent than that you "always wanted to write." Too many writers say that to impress anyone in the publishing business. Use the space in your one-page letter to tell the agent that you've taken writing classes, published a poem or spent ten years honing your marketing skills to prepare for the publishing adventure ahead. You're trying to sell your writing (and yourself) here!

Participle *ings* are not a gerund's twin

Your **Find** utility will also pick out the *ing* in a sentence like "Writing from the age of five, I became interested in telling the story of the culture I was raised in." *Writing* here is a participle or a verb that screws itself up to describe something—in this case to describe the verb of the independent clause. The entire first clause is a modifier and tells when the action happened. It could easily have morphed into a clause that describes a noun.

One of the problems many of the sentences using participles have —and they tend to have a lot—is that they don't relate well to the rest of the sentence. In this case, the age of the writer is not that pertinent to either the meaning or the tone of the independent clause.

A construction of this kind may result from the author trying to pack too many bits of information into a sentence. A gatekeeper will not only notice, she'll yawn.

Your sentences with participles in them may not be as bad as the example I've given, but you get the idea. A sentence like my participle example can be edited in myriad ways. Certainly, "I became interested in telling the story of the culture I was raised in," might work even though a few meticulous grammarians like Strunk and White wouldn't like to see the sentence end with a preposition. So, in the interest of not offending a gatekeeper, you might try, "Early on I became interested in . . . " Or, if you must get that early age into the mix, "I began to write when I was five and soon became interested in . . . " might do the trick.

Try several edits on for size to see which is more to the point, moves the sentence along better, is more dramatic or whatever it is you're trying to achieve.

You may need to practice using your **Find Function** a bit. Using it is like running a fine-toothed comb through your copy, but only you will be able to pick apart the sentences your *ings* occur in to see if they're effective (rarely) and decide how to fix them.

Was-ing and were-ing

I have become intimately involved with a Brit. Whenever I'm on the freeway with nothing to do but drive, Michel Thomas teaches me Spanish with his series of CDs. He may have been the one to coin the phrase "wuzzing and whirring," but he uses this term because he dislikes using scary grammar terms. In spite of the fact that I just hit you with awful words like *gerunds* and *participles*, I hate to use them, too.

In this discussion of *was-ing* and *were-ing*, I'm not going to do that. Suffice it to say that most of us use the helper verbs *was*, *were*, *have* and a few others when the simple past would do just fine. That is true when writing nonfiction, but we all tend to use helpers when they are unnecessary. Use your **Find Function** to examine each and every one of them and see if you can eradicate a few.

Here's an example from one of my early query letters: "*This Is the Place* has won eight awards." Really? How does the word *has* clarify tense? The book *won* the awards, plain and simple. The action is over and done with. Why drag on a poor agent's ears with needless *hases, haves* and their cousins?

48

14 ≈ Edit Your Idiosyncrasies

Though your **Find Function** is not a therapist, it can help you with your personal oddities. I overuse *just. A Cup of Comfort* author JayCe Crawford watches for *euphemistically*, of all things. Use your Find feature and evaluate your favorites both in terms of frequency and effectiveness. Don't let your attachment to these words keep you from using the delete button. Your editor—the one provided by your publisher or the one you hire (unless you're being stubborn or . . . er, inordinately frugal)—will not be as familiar with your writing eccentricities as you are if you have taken the time to analyze your own writing patterns.

What Fun! Your Own Dictionary!

Go to **Tools** on your toolbar, then **Options**, then the **Spelling and Grammar** tab, then the little button that says **Customize dictionaries**.

Learn more about Word's Custom Dictionary process at
www.kerryr.net/webwriting/tools_custom-dicts.htm.

The tutorial includes step-by-step instructions for all versions of Word. You'll find tips on changing your custom dictionary here: www.worldstart.com/tips/tips.php/1128.

If you are working with a vocabulary all your own—a dialect, accent or jargon—create a custom dictionary in Word to be sure

Carolyn Howard-Johnson

that you use the same spelling for a specific term every time. Word will let you create up to ten dictionaries for your own needs.

If your character uses *sez* for *says*, you won't want to spell it *sayz*. The decision is yours as to which is correct and your custom dictionary will pick up any variation

Ready made science, jargon and dialect dictionaries are available as books and as computer programs. For recommendations, see the links in Appendix Three of this book. To find others, Google "custom dictionary" +(use the plus symbol) and then (type the subject you are looking for here). If you need more help with Web research tools (known by the experts as Boolean logic), see the index for a series of tapes produced by the Audio Divas for Double Dragon Publishing.

15 ≋ Let Word Help You Analyze Your Copy

The spelling checker has two valuable tools attached that some authors avoid or have never seen. They are the **Readability Statistics** and **Word Count** boxes. They are the old gray matrons who help keep you in line. Either can be used for word count and both are invaluable for writers when they have a word limit. However, the more useful of the two is the Readability Statistics box, for it has dozens of uses other than making your document fit an editor's space requirements. For example:

- Young adult and children's book authors use it to target a specific grade level.

- Journalists and freelancers use it to keep their copy within the reading range of a periodical's audience.

- James Patterson may use it to keep his paragraphs no more than two sentences in length. In other words, this tool can help you with certain aspects of pacing your story.

- My own favorite is using it to keep passive construction working to clarify tense and not to slow copy to a pace where readers will want to nap.

16 ≋ Wipe Out Your Ineffective Passives

Speaking of passive, you will want to assess how you use it in everything you write. It's not that the passive tense doesn't have its place. It's that when it is overused your sentences may become wordy and ungainly. Overuse may even cause your readers to nod off.

Passive tense does allow the writer to clarify time sequences and to avoid providing a subject for the verb. That quirk allows politicians (and others) to avoid direct apologies. At most, the passive is just plain dreadful. Volumes have been written on the subject, and if you need to know more about them, look it up. Here are two fine resources:

> **Easy Test to Keep Passives from Inducing a Snooze**
>
> Is the subject of the sentence doing anything or is it having something done to it? The latter is —obviously—passive. Examples: "Tony is editing my manuscript," is active.
>
> "My manuscript is being edited by Tony," is passive.

Purdue University's take on the passive is clearly illustrated and they give excellent examples of when passive may be preferred at: http://owl.english.purdue.edu/handouts/grammar/g_actpass.html.

Rutgers University gives examples of how politicos and others use passive to weasel out of stuff; you may find them amusing and edifying: http://andromeda.rutgers.edu/~jlynch/Writing/p.html.

Carolyn Howard-Johnson

Understanding how passive verbs may be manipulated in this way may help if you're writing dialogue for a wimp, if you are intentionally slowing the pace of your work, or if you want to place your story in an earlier time when language and life were less hurried.

Your **Grammar Checker** and **Find Function** can help you look through your manuscript to evaluate passive construction. For an evaluation-at-a-glance, let your spelling and grammar checker take you directly to your Readability Statistics box when you have finished your check (see the sidebar for directions on how to make it do that for you). There, in the bottom section, you will find both your **Flesch Readability Ease** and your **Passive Sentences** scores. The latter will let you know immediately how successful you were at keeping the passive voice out of your work or—for very good reasons—putting it in.

How to Automate Your Readability Statistics Box

Go to your toolbar and:

- Click on **Tools**.
- Click on **Options**.
- Click on the **Spelling and Grammar** tab.
- In the second section down, put a check in the box by **Show Readability Statistics**.
- Be sure you click the **OK** button to make the change permanent.

17 ≋ You're an Author: You Get to Change Your Mind!

Authors often use the name of a real person to model a character. Then, as they are editing, they come up with a name that is more suitable. Leora Krygier, author of *When She Sleeps*, found it necessary to change the names of her characters twice. Something similar can occur with company names, place names and others.

Whenever you make an across-the-board modification, be careful that you change every occurrence individually. If you choose to use the **Find and Replace** function, you run the risk of missing places where the name has been shortened or typed incorrectly. The Replace process may also change the original name in places where a short name like *Ted* is contained within a longer word. The gremlins love the Replace Function that changes everything in its path that is a match. You won't be as fond of it as they are when you see what it can do to your copy.

As a double check, you might take groups of three or four letters and run a second check to be sure all the changes were made. For the name *Christy*, you might run *Chris* and *isty* finds.

You might also change your mind about matters of style that require replacing earlier style choices. Generally publishers use a stylebook to guide them with such decisions. The most used are the *Associated Press Stylebook* and the *Chicago Manual of Style*. If you write fiction, *Garner's Modern American Usage* is a good addition. Fiction requirements may differ. For example, guidelines for spelling out numbers are less casual for novels, so treat some of your style choices like medical decisions; get several opinions. I listed other references for you in Appendix Three.

If you are writing a novel that includes language from a specific discipline, don't neglect researching their jargon and syntax. You will want a discipline-specific style guide to confirm your choices. You may want input from a field person to double-check them.

We occasionally find the stylebooks disagree or don't take a position on new words. In those cases, we may need to make judgment calls. An example of style choices you may have to make on your own is the word *website*. The *Los Angeles Times* and hundreds of publications both online and in print use it the way I chose to for this book. Perhaps more accurately, because *Web* is capitalized when it stands alone, the *New York Times* uses *Web site*. The first approach is becoming so common that I find the great New York newspaper's style a bit jarring and, as authors, we don't want to jolt our readers out of the mood we are trying to create.

Remember *bussing*? Eventually most agreed on *busing*, much to my chagrin. The latter defies the rules of spelling we all once learned. By all rules of pronunciation *busing* should be pronounced *bewsing*, and we don't need anything more in our language to confuse the spelling-challenged. You know my mantra, though. Once common usage determines an accepted protocol, you don't want to raise the ire of a gatekeeper by challenging it.

For this book, I decided on *e-book* over *ebook*, and *e-mail* over *email*. I figure that if *e* stands for *electronic* then it would be *electronic book* or *electronic-book*, not electronicbook. That's my stand. You may stand on another platform altogether. Once the big guys make a choice, it's best to go along with it, especially when the acceptance of our work may be at stake; it looks as if my position on *e-book* and *e-mail* may be as soundly trounced as the stand I took on *bussing*. Sometimes frequency trumps what is rational.

In this book, *The Frugal Editor*, I decided to capitalize Find Function rather than italicize it although I do make it bold when I want you to apply it to a specific process. I used the Find Function to go back and make those changes after I made that momentous decision. That's when I ran into trouble. What if I wanted some of the entries of those two words to be in bold face? *Find* is a common word and can even be found within words. What if the gremlins were working on an exigency I hadn't considered? I decided to follow my own advice and let the Find Function help me do the changes one at a time and skip the Find and Replace function that could play havoc with my new style choice.

An important defense against gremlins is a style sheet. When you've made a style decision, jot it down or make a note in a separate file on your computer. Alphabetize the entries. This attention to detail will save you research time. You won't notice so much if you make a style sheet, but if you don't, you'll be kicking yourself for not utilizing this easy method for keeping straight all those puny details your brain will refuse to track.

18 ∾ Code Words Served Batman: They Can Serve You, Too

When our memories fail we can use codes to designate an elusive word or concept. When we need to do more research we can use the same code or a different one. JayCe Crawford couldn't think of the name for an old-time restaurant called DuPar's Deli in Glendale, California, a Los Angeles area community. She used *Jerry's* as a temporary substitute every time she wanted to refer to the restaurant by name. When she finally remembered, she used the **Find Function** to replace *Jerry's*. I prefer a series of XXXs, because it's easy to run a find on three Xs, and if I should miss making a change, any editor will notice my faux pas.

19 ∾ Viruses Aren't the Only Communicable Diseases Contracted from the Net

Webmasters, bloggers and e-zine editors must work quickly. The Internet and the ease of publishing fast may lead us astray. What we see in print is often carelessly written and we see some errors so frequently we come to believe they are not mistakes.

The Net is not solely to blame for these errors. They are so frequently made that we have come to ignore them. And we've come to emulate them. We must take responsibility for our own craft. We also must realize that language changes. So to assume that because we once learned something one way, it will always be accepted is fallacious. To neglect researching the language we write in when we so assiduously research the facts for what we write is folly. On the next few pages I talk about some of the other communicable diseases many of us have contracted in addition to the overuse of capitals and italics that you changed in your manual edit.

Quotation marks used for emphasis or for cute

Unfortunately, much of our writing has been infected with the quotation mark virus that encourages sloppy writing. Even though some of the edits in this section may be made more accurately on your hardcopy, your **Find Function** can also be used as an effective prescription against them. It will easily find quotation marks in your text for you; it is up to you whether you want to edit them manually or use your FF or a combination of both.

I know. You can't imagine how quotation marks could be giving you trouble. Therefore I'm going to plead with you not to skip this section. Plead! For you it will be just a review and, if it turns out you needed it worse than you thought, you can e-mail me later to thank me for getting down on my knees to you.

Quotation Mark No-Nos

- Other than around some titles do not use quotation marks with words not being spoken by a character. (See the "A Few Helpers for Punctuating Dialogue" sidebar in Section III for more tips on editing dialogue.)

- That a phrase is also a title or appears on a sign somewhere does not give one carte blanche to play freely with quotation marks. (Imagine the embarrassment of doing this incorrectly on a sign at a writers' fair!) See the sidebar "Titles Are Tattletales" in chapter eight for more on quotation marks.

- Do not use quotation marks around any word that will be understood without them.

- Do not use them around colloquialisms or slang.

- Do not use them around numbers or letters for which the symbols rather than the written words are used. Like CD or TV.

- Use italics rather than quotation marks to indicate that a word stands for itself. Example: "The word *ditch* can be used colloquially to mean *avoid*."

When I was attending a master class provided for the UCLA Extension Writers' Program instructors, one of our most popular teachers bemoaned the use of quotation marks around words that are merely slang and not irony or sarcasm. He pointed out that this is a mark of the amateur. He suggested that if a reader will understand your meaning without the quotation marks, ditch them. Notice I didn't put any quotation marks around the word *ditch*? I apologize for not crediting this instructor but I've "forgotten" who it was. Yes, with those quotation marks around *forgotten*, I'm showing that I really haven't forgotten at all but am more than likely a little miffed with my associate for exploding a favorite writers' affectation.

Avoid the inclination to use italics to replace the quotation marks you've eradicated. The reader will know what a word means, even if you use it colloquially. In fact a word is colloquial when many come to use it differently from its more formal meaning. That would include your reader. You needn't point out what he already knows. He may, in fact, be insulted that you thought so little of his reading ability.

So, we've covered a couple of the most irritating quotation mark blunders. There is an array of them. A quotation mark in your copy can be a magic indicator, one that will help you ream out many offenses that the gremlins would like you to ignore.

You'll want to check chapter twenty-four — "Dialogue Migraines" and the sidebar in this chapter for other quotation mark transgressions.

Question marks and exclamation points running amok

Question marks and exclamation points are fun in e-mails. With them, we can make a point without taking pains to make our writing concise. You'll want to avoid using multiples of either of these punctuation marks in your writing. This is a good place to use your **Find Function**. Check each one out when your head is clear and ditch the multiples. Let it be an occasion to reconsider each mark. Most of us let the fun of them lure us into overuse.

20 ≋ Enhance Your Characterization and Dialogue

Use the **Find Function** not only to correct but to enhance. Leora Krygier imagined a character for her novel *Finding Maynard*. This character uses the word *except* as an indication of an indecisive personality. Krygier uses her FF to trace the *except*s in that character's dialogue. She checks to make sure she uses the word enough to help the reader subconsciously identify this speech pattern with the character but not so much that the process itself will become noticeable to the reader. You may want to use this technique for your characters' other idiosyncrasies, not only their speech but their physical mannerisms.

21 ≋ Find Your Ellipsis Dots Gone Wild

I n *Writing Dialogue,* Tom Chiarella suggests writers use ellipses to indicate natural pauses in dialogue or an interruption. (Of course they're also used to indicate a section of a quotation that has been removed to accommodate space limitation or to aid understanding.) An ellipsis is three periods — no fewer, no more. If it comes at the end of a sentence, you may find four dots, but one of them is a period.

To fix these, use your **Find Function**. Type two periods into the **Find What** box. It will find both those that suffer from sticky key syndrome and contain more than three as well as those that have been shortchanged.

Also check to see if you have over-used ellipses. After all, they don't really say anything. An instructor at the Association of Mormon Letters Writers' Conference I spoke at noted that there is little room for ellipses in poetry (where language should be condensed). Use them only when, as an example, the lack of language says much more than the language itself would say or when you are purging words unneeded for your purpose.

You will find more on formatting ellipses in chapter thirty-two — "Check Up on Your Formatter."

Making Possessives So Simple the Gremlin Can't Fool with You

- Add *'s* to a singular form of the word, even if it ends in *s*. Example: *Travis's uniform*. (Yes, the stylebooks do disagree on this and there are what I call seat-of-the-pants exceptions. Sound seems to be the determiner, or an individual publisher or journal's style guidelines.)

- Add *'s* to plural forms that do not end in *s*. Example: *children's*.

- Add only the apostrophe to the end of plural nouns that end in *s*: Example: *several eggs' yolks* or *writers' program*.

- Add *'s* only to the end-syllable in compound words. Example: *sister-in-law's children*.

- Add *'s* only to the last noun in a series to show joint possession of a single object. Example: *Nancy and Ted's house*. Rarely two people will possess two items; in that case each of the owners would get a separate little marker for a possessive. Example: *Nancy's and Ted's cars*.

- Do not add an apostrophe to a possessive pronoun. The words yours, theirs, his, etc., already indicate possession. In this case, the gremlin usually coaxes you into an error only when you have a prepositional phrase. Example: *He is an enemy of yours* (not *an enemy of yours'* or *your's*).

Note: These rules may be slightly different—especially the rules with plurals—from the ones you learned in school. The updated ones are easier. Rejoice!

68

22 ≋ The Frightful Apostrophes

We use apostrophes to form possessives, to form the plurals of some lowercase letters and to indicate the omission of letters. Gremlins love to tease us with them. If we want to foil the fifteen-fingered guy, we need to know the rules and carefully examine each use during the editing process. Your **Find Function** will serve up every single one for your inspection.

Possessives

Purdue University's website (http://owl.english.purdue.edu/handouts/grammar) gives a simple rule for the use of possessives, one we all may know. They suggest that we, "turn the suspected phrase around and make it an 'of the . . . phrase'" in order to know for sure.

Example: the gremlin's nasty habit = the nasty habit of the gremlin. Don't use the passive construction, though! This is just a test. Testing . . . Testing . . .

Though you know the rule and would spot any infraction of that rule in a split second if it were in someone else's copy, you may not in your own. When our fingers type, they sometimes stick things in where they don't belong. Sometimes our brains misfire. At any rate, you'll want to look at each apostrophe. Once you determine that you need a possessive, use the rules in the sidebar to be absolutely surefire correct.

Apostrophes that don't form plurals

We're all tired of seeing apostrophes used incorrectly to make plurals. Native English speakers know gremlins have been laboring overtime, but because we are so familiar with our language we forget that there are times when apostrophes are used to make plurals. No kidding! See the first entry in the sidebar "Sneaky Uses of Apostrophes."

Most of us know these rules, but we do slip occasionally. A **Find Function** search will let you examine each one to be sure momentary apostropheitis did not cause you to type in one of the little brats where it doesn't belong.

Sorry, but if you sometimes forget to use apostrophes where they're required, you'll have to rely on the old manual editing approach. For that, go through your copy and check every word. To be thorough, you could use the FF to do a search on all words that end in *s* by keying *s*(space) in the find box.

Sneaky Uses of Apostrophes

- Use apostrophes to form plurals of lowercase letters. We all know the rule to mind our *p's* and *q's*.

- Use apostrophes to indicate an omission of letters. Contractions are an example. Another is when you drop letters to indicate casual enunciation or dialect. Warning: *Till* is a word. Do not reason that it is a shortened version of *until* that would need an apostrophe if it were. Another caution: *Could've* (or *could have*) is correct, not *could of*.

- Use special care with *its* and *it's*. *Its* is the possessive form and *it's* is the contraction. Ditto with *your* and *you're*. *Your* is the possessive.

- Do not use apostrophes to form plurals of capital letters, numbers or symbols. This, too, is a new, simplified grammar rule, so you'll see examples of apostrophes used this way in older books or formal or academic papers. Now your editor will prefer *ATMs, Zs, 3s,* and *&s*.

---

23 ∿ You're a Writer: You Get to Make Up Words

Sometimes we make up words that sound like something we've heard (someone made up *tick-tock* a long time ago). Sometimes we form new words by connecting two as if they were one or by attaching prefixes or suffixes. Those don't cause us too many problems. It's when we start fooling with hyphens that we run into trouble. If you have a good reason for doing so have at it. A good reason is generally one that can be articulated but should, in most cases, be backed by a rationale better than ones I sometimes hear from my students. Reasons like "I just like it better that way," or, "I want to be different."

Your Spelling Checker Does Know the Difference Between One Word and Two

Here's how to force your spelling checker to give you better direction than it otherwise would. Push together two words that look as if they might be one word. Watch for that angry little red squiggle. *Oldfashioned* gets the red alert; *foolproof* doesn't. Yet both register as correct when left as two words.

Now try the same pairs using a hyphen. Both *old-fashioned* and *fool-proof* come out with no notifier. The spelling checker helped in the first case but not in the second. You see, even Word doesn't want to get into the to-hyphenate-or-not-to-hyphenate fray.

Carolyn Howard-Johnson

It's your prerogative to change even words that are clearly spelled out for you in a good dictionary. Here are two examples that confuse not only my spelling checker in Word but also the one in my e-mail program:

- This is an example of an intentionally hyphenated word that would normally not be hyphenated. It's from "Earliest Remembered Sound" in my chapbook of poetry, *Tracings*:

> Father wears a military cap,
> grosgrain ribbons
> across his heart;
> smells of gabardine
> and *good-byes.*

My reason for hyphenating good-byes was that I wanted the careful reader to see the poignant and positive quality in even a painful goodbye—without explaining the concept.

- Here's an example of putting two words together without the hyphen from "Everywhere My Dream," a poem in the same book:

> I followed my *childman*
> beyond a young girl's borders
> calling nowhere home . . .

If you're not in your creative mode (or in the mood to confound editors or gremlins) see the sidebar "Quick Test for Hyphenating Double Adjectives" for guidelines. When in doubt research like crazy, because guidelines are not always clear and hyphens are used (and not used) in so many ways. Beyond that, you may need to be brave when you're in your poetic or literary mode. Be cautious when you're approaching gatekeepers.

Because the rules of hyphenating are so intricate and because even the experts disagree, the hyphen gremlin (one of the most spiteful of his species) knows that he can have a field day with them.

Hyphens (as well as the passive voice) can cause more arguments among otherwise tolerant people than they are worth. Therefore, don't write to me to tell me I'm wrong. You are free to disagree. My only firm rule is to research the subject and the individual occurrence before using a hyphen and to be open to a different opinion (but not submissive to that opinion). On some things— even when we are trying to impress gatekeepers—there is no such thing as a zero-tolerance rule in spite of what Truss would have us believe.

Use your **Find Function** but not your spelling checker to do a final check on hyphens just before you send your work off to where it will be perused by a critical (and professional) pair of eyes. Where hyphens are concerned, your checker is as confused as a copy editor with a hangover. FF will find your hyphenated words, but from there you are on your own.

> ### Quick Test for Hyphenating Double Adjectives
>
> Place an *and* between the two adjectives you are considering. If it feels right, both adjectives modify the noun. In that case, no hyphen is needed. Example:
>
> *He is an exacting, proud editor.*
>
> *He is an exacting and proud editor.*
>
> There is a difference in style between the two but no loss in meaning in either case.
>
> *He is a detail oriented editor.*
>
> *He is a detail and oriented editor.*
>
> Oops. Obviously detail modifies oriented, not editor. Use the hyphen.
>
> *He is a detail-oriented editor.*

73

Playing Peek-a-Boo with Hyphens

- You may occasionally ignore hyphens to make whole new words.

- Use hyphens to separate syllables at the ends of printed lines. These aren't often problems because Word and other programs wrap lines for you—usually, if not always, accurately.

- Use hyphens to separate some prefixes from root words.

- Do not use hyphens to separate suffixes from root words. (Just to make the subject more confusing, there may be a time when using a hyphen with suffixes will clarify your meaning.) *Business-ese*, is an example. I chose to use the hyphen for this book. I kind of made up the word anyway and it seemed better with the hyphen than without, perhaps because of the two *s* sounds; I decided to go with my own assessment for clarity over the rulebook. An editor may indeed be watching but I already have a publisher.

- Use hyphens to aid understanding when more than one word is used to modify a noun. Only sometimes. Only when they come before the noun, not after. Example: *well-known author* or *The author is well known.*

- This site shows how using a hyphen (or not) can change your meaning: www.grammar-monster.com/lessons/lhyphen.htm

Hyphens and Prefixes Are in Cahoots with the Gremlins

- Some say when you attach a prefix to a word that's not listed in the dictionary with that prefix, there is no need to use a hyphen.

- Many grammarians say that when a common prefix—the key word here is *common*—is attached to a word there is no need for a hyphen. That includes prefixes like *co* or *post.*

- Others say if a word is not listed in the dictionary with the prefix, use a hyphen.

- Because there are so few firm rules governing using prefixes with root words, I say if the word you invented looks funny either together or separated, put in a hyphen to see how it looks that way. Go for the one that feels right or makes the meaning clearer. (cont'd)

74

Here are some less flexible rules:

- Use a hyphen when attaching a prefix to a number or capitalized word. Examples: *Pre-1920s. Pre-Thanksgiving*.

- Use a hyphen when attaching a prefix to a word that is already hyphenated. June Casagrande, author of *Grammar Snobs Are Great Big Meanies*, gives the example *non-self-serving*.

- When your hyphenated word shoves two vowels together, separate them with a hyphen. Exceptions are commonly used words like *cooperate*.

- When adding a prefix to multi-word compounds, use a longer punctuation called an en-dash (a longer dash, sort of two hyphens connected. You can set your Word program to do that for you automatically when you type two hyphens.) *Post World War II* would become *Post(hyphen hyphen)World War II*. En-dashes are also used for designating periods of years:
  1980(en-dash)1990.
  They are also used to indicate opposition. An example:
  urban(en-dash)agrarian.
  Make an en-dash by holding down the **ALT** key on your keyboard and typing 0150 on your **number pad**.

- Unless you attach the prefix *non* to a proper noun, don't use a hyphen. It's *nonsequitur, nonfiction*.

- Avoid the hyphen when you feel inclined to connect an adverb that ends in *ly* to another word. Casagrande uses *happily married couple* as an example. The idea is that *ly* already lets you know it is married (as it were) to the word *married*.

Note: For a more rigid take on hyphens read Lynne Truss's *Eats, Shoots & Leaves, The Zero Tolerance Approach to Punctuation*. She is a Brit and the British publishers follow different grammar, spelling and style rules from ours. The Harry Potter books had their own American editions.

24 ≈≈ Dialogue Migraines

Warning here! If you write nonfiction only, don't skip over this section. More nonfiction writers are using dialogue than ever before. It's now found in news stories in our nation's most-respected newspapers. Journalists interested in straight, unbiased news realize the value of dialogue for sparking up their articles.

The danger here is that, unless you — writer of fiction or nonfiction — have read a lot of fiction in the past and have a mind for absorbing the nuances of what you see on a page, you may get it wrong. Miserably wrong.

Your reader wouldn't be able to do much better, of course, but she'll know something is amiss because she's been trained to expect certain dialogue indicators and forms since she learned to read. If a writer wings it, her reader will sense it. Even if a writer intentionally deviates from guidelines, that reader will be taken out of the story by the departure in style.

Punctuation migraine

The Internet, stylebooks and some popular experimental writers have begun to influence punctuation rules.

Tara Ison uses no quotation marks around some dialogue in *The List*. Earlier, Frank McCourt chose to break with quotation mark tradition, and he tends to report what his characters say in his narrative more frequently than many writers. McCourt writes memoirs. This style suits memoirs better than some other genres but, even then, many found McCourt's departures not simpler but a distraction—at least at first. Readers have, after all, been trained to ignore the conventions of dialogue and they haven't been taught to ignore variations from them.

The source of an apparent error is not important when your query or manuscript is facing a gatekeeper. An agent or editor will not care whether you chose to depart from generally accepted guidelines for punctuating dialogue, made errors out of ignorance or a gremlin attacked your copy. It is that acceptance you're after, not winning a quibble over dialogue etiquette with the person judging your submission.

I worry when one of my editing clients becomes adamant over a matter of opinion or taste, especially when she or he deserves a key to that door to success. It is best to know the rules for dialogue, abide by them and change them (if you must) only after your work has been accepted or once you are known and don't have to get by an arbiter of any kind. See the sidebar "Punctuating Dialogue" for some essential guidelines.

A Few Helpers for Punctuating Dialogue

Here are a few guidelines for using punctuation that won't chill an editor's ardor. We all know the basic rules:

- Introduce dialogue after a standard dialogue tag with a comma.
  John said, "Please help me with my dialogue."

- Use a colon to introduce a quotation after an independent clause.
  This is what John says we should do to edit dialogue tags: "Go very slowly. Check them one by one."

- Capitalize the first letter within the quotation as if the sentence began there. For the speaker of the dialogue, it does begin there.   (cont'd)

Here's where—too often—we get confused:

- A period ends a sentence and always goes inside the quotation marks that come after the sentence.

  John said, "If anything comes up that is not covered by these few guidelines, even a good editor may have to research ways to punctuate around quotation marks."

- Commas, too, go inside the quotation marks. Always.

  "Even a good editor," John said, "may have to research some arcane grammar rules." (The second comma in the sentence is governed by the first rule in this sidebar.)

- Exclamation points, question marks, semicolons and even dashes go within the quotation marks when they apply to the quotation itself. Put them outside the quotation marks when they apply to the whole sentence.

  John shook his fist. "I hate it that way!"

  Or "I don't care what you think about Jane's calmly saying, 'I don't care for that'!" See how the exclamation point comes outside of what Jane says calmly? In this example, it is the speaker who is vehement, not Jane, who happens to be calm.

- Colons, by default, go outside quotation marks, and if I do say so, look as if gremlins have been at work, probably because the rule is so frequently ignored. Just trust me. Even if you think a colon should be inside the curly guys, put it outside.

- If you should need to use parentheses at the end of the sentence and after a quotation, the period goes after the parenthetical expression. You may need to use something like this example for a proposal:

  N. B. Harrow says, "Memoirs about drug addiction are on the upswing since Frey's fiasco" (see www.writingtrends.com for the original source).

Intrusive tags headaches

Make your dialogue tags—the "he saids" and "she saids"—disappear when possible. When you must use tags for clarity, those "he saids" and "she saids" are standard—usually the preferred—

tags. Anything more creative draws attention to itself. Avoid variations on the tried and true. If your character whines, the reader should know it from what that character says, the context she finds herself in (the setting) and the reaction of the person she is speaking to. To use the word *whine* would then not only be conspicuous but also redundant.

The guidelines are a little less stringent for nonfiction, but writers will still want to avoid diverting readers' attention away from their purpose by deviating from the conventions they have come to accept—and to ignore.

Use the **Find Function** in Word to check your dialogue tags and your punctuation. Check every single occurrence. In each case consider the rules in the sidebar box one by one. You can use this same check to see if you've overworked your dialogue tags. Don't use tags when voice and other cues will do the job. Punctuation considerations more intricate than these can usually be avoided; by doing so you'll circumvent the rare occasion when an agent thinks she knows correct usage but doesn't and (yikes!) judges your correct choice as incorrect.

In *On Writing* Stephen King tells us that a dialogue tag can dictate the use of punctuation in the dialogue itself. For instance, if the tag uses a form of the word *ask,* avoid using a question mark with the quotation marks. We're trying to avoid being redundant.

> He asked, "How old are you." or
> He said, "How old are you?" or, with no tag,
> "How old are you?"

It may seem like a small thing, but an agent or editor might actually give you points for knowing it.

Section IV
Final Housecleaning

25 ≋ More Editing Ahead

I can't see you, but I know you are rolling your eyes or tapping your fingers. Two manual edits and all those tricks with the computer aren't enough? When you've gone through the next few steps you may not understand why what you've done is not sufficient, but you will know that it isn't.

26 ≋ You're B-a-a-a-ck: Two Final, Manual Edits

Neither of your two final reads should be on your computer screen.

Print out your manuscript single spaced because that is close to how it will eventually look on a printed page. Do a quick scan of each page for odd spacing, paragraph indents, etc., and then read it once over carefully in this format. Use a colored pen for corrections. Yes, you will find some errors. Make those corrections one at a time in your electronic copy.

Now you get to do it again. This time double space. That's the format in which your manuscript will be submitted. Your query or cover letter will appear single spaced in its final form, so looking at it in double space will work to your advantage. You will see specific grammar boo-boos, typos—even style changes—in both these versions that you didn't see before.

You will get a better feel for:

- Flow.

- Transitions, character, time and location.

- Dialogue patterns.

- Typos.

- Misuse of synonyms and other closely aligned words. For help with specific words of this kind, turn to this book's Appendix Two and to Barbara McNichol's site for her free handbooks and services. You will find her at www.barbaramcnichol.com.

- Repetition. (Yes, even after the electronic search!)

- How your chapter titles, chapter divisions, subtitles, and the other two-by-fours that frame your book are working. Your titles and other divisions must exactly match the table of contents.

- If you plan to publish certain kinds of nonfiction traditionally, your editor will request an index. If you are self- or subsidy-publishing nonfiction that needs an index, this is the time to make one or commission one.

These final read-throughs are needed for a couple of reasons. Aside from the fact that gremlins will have been working on your manuscript as you were editing (they never sleep), the cleaner the copy, the more likely you are to see both the abstruse and ordinary errors that were hidden before.

Get a little help from your friends

Do you have a critique group or a writing friend you can enlist to help? Ask one of them to go over your manuscript for you.

Do you know someone who likes reading in your genre? Ask him or her to help out, too.

One is an expert, the other your target audience. You can learn from each reader and now that your manuscript is clean, you won't be embarrassed to have them look at it. You'll have two pairs of fresh new eyes and two new viewpoints.

Having these two edits (or more) done at once can save time, though you may find that tangential input gives better results because edits layered on top of edits may be more finely tuned.

If your reader is comfortable with computers, let him or her edit using the **Track** in your word processing program. (See instructions on how to use **TRK** in chapter two — "Organizing Only Feels

Like Procrastination.") Use track's color-coding feature so you know who made specific suggestions.

If using amateur editors is new to you, be wary of those who overreach to the point of wanting to restyle your book. Give each of your helpmates some guidelines, but if they overstep, don't take offense. This is your creation. Take what you can use and discard the rest. Be equally wary of being so set in your ways that you don't listen.

Don't forget to add these helpers' names to your acknowledgments. Each will appreciate a complimentary copy upon the book's release. It's the least you can do.

Extra Spaces Are Like Fluff Balls Under the Bed

You may not be able to see the extra spaces in your copy, but they can cause havoc when your manuscript is converted into a finished product. Here's how to get rid of them.

Click on the **Paragraph Icon** (¶) in your Word screen. It should be in the top row of your **toolbar** unless some computer-proficient type has fooled around with your options. It looks like a backward **P** with the little half circle colored in. Suddenly you'll be able to see all the directions you gave your copy as you typed. One little *dot* will appear in your manuscript for every time you used your **Spacebar**. All you have to do is use your **backspace** key to delete the unnecessary ones.

27 ≈ Dust Off the Cobwebs

Final cleanup is a breeze. It's a little like using Endust. It picks up most of the small, less-evident particles in your copy. The process will make it easier for an editor to spot wayward errors and easier for a formatter to make your pages look spiffy.

To do this last edit, you need to know how your computer is thinking. To set up your document for this task, see the "Spot the Dots" sidebar. Don't panic when little paragraph marks (¶) and dots appear all over your pages. When you toggle the icon, they will disappear.

This book can't cover all of the formatting that needs to be done; unless you are self-publishing and choose not to hire a formatter, you won't need to know everything about the process, anyway. Instead, I've covered the parts that some publishers expect of their authors. Also—frugally speaking—if you are self-publishing, your formatter may give you a price break if you tell him that you'll do some of the preliminaries yourself.

Eliminate pesky single spaces

Let's start with the spaces we stick in there out of habit when we click on the **Spacebar** at the end of a paragraph. We do this because it feels like (because it is) the end of a sentence. Go back through the entire document. Inspect the end of every paragraph. Delete any little dots you find there, other than periods or other punctuation.

Slim those chubby spaces between sentences

If you learned to type on an old-fashioned typewriter, as I did, you may tap the **Spacebar** twice between sentences. Computers do something called kerning for you these days. Kerning is the process of proportionately spacing wide and narrow letters on the page so only a single tap is necessary. If you learned to type recently, you probably only tap the **Spacebar** once between sentences, but all the rest of us need to go back and erase any little excess **Spacebar** dots. Except for those writing their dissertations or other academic work, the battle cry is "Only one space dot between sentences, please!"

Use your **Find Function** to weed out these double dots or do it manually.

Let Your Find Function Spot the Dots

By now you know how to use your **Find Function**. Select the **Replace** tab. Place your cursor in the **Find what** window and tap your **Spacebar** twice. It will appear you have typed nothing. In the **Replace with** window, you'll tap the **Spacebar** only once. Now select the third button over from the left at the bottom of the window that reads **Replace All** and click. Voilà! Even with two apparently blank windows you will have sent a message to your computer's brain to replace all the double spacing in your document—whether between words or between sentences—with single spacing.

Caution: Before you tap your **Spacebar**, be sure your **cursor** is as far to the left of the window as it can go. To do that, backspace until the little bar can go no farther left before entering your invisible spaces.

---

28 ⚏ Your Final Spelling and Grammar Check

The final **spelling and grammar check** on your computer is an important one. You probably have yours turned on as you work, or you set it to active mode during the preliminary edit. I know a few authors who find their speller an intrusion on their writing process. Even those who trust their own skills more than they do the automated checker (and they should) will want to run their document through a final check. If you aren't proficient in Word, you'll find how to do it in the "Your Flawed Friend" sidebar earlier in chapter two, "Organizing Only Feels Like Procrastination."

This final spelling and grammar check will help you reevaluate lots of specifics in your document. It is excellent at some things. For example, it will pick up the correct plural spellings of all nouns that end in *o*. Should that word end in *es* or plain old *s*? This your spell checker knows for sure.

The **spelling checker** will pause where its computer brain thinks there is a spelling or grammar error. You choose to accept the change it suggests or not. Here are some reminders that will make the task easier:

- This function isn't an editor and it won't sense as many errors as you'd think its little automated brain should. It will be up to you to fine-tune your piece—and you've already done that.

- Read the **prompt** at the top of the window. It will tell you why it has selected the passage it shows in the window. If you neglect that little indicator, you may not understand why the computer has stopped there and correct for something else, or, just as bad, assume all is well with what you are looking at.

- Don't let yourself get too tired. If this exercise becomes perfunctory, the gremlins will seize the advantage.

- Resist the temptation to keep clicking on the **Ignore** button.

And guess what? Microsoft is working on a program that will conjugate verbs for us. I haven't tested it or seen it but this is a tool most editors and authors will want to add to their battery of checking aids. Checking aids. Band-Aids. This will, after all, be a computer program. Just like the other checkers and helps, it will not cure but it may make boo-boos less likely to turn into infections. You'll still have to let it point out possible trouble and make up your own mind about the validity of anything it finds.

29 ⚐ Are You Convinced You Need an Editor?

I will understand if after all this hard work, you think your editing is done and you don't need to partner with an editor, at least not before you hand your manuscript over to a publisher who will assign one of theirs to you.

On the other hand, all this work may convince you that you do need an editor. You may come to realize that you have only scratched the surface. Perhaps you decide to self-, small-press-, or subsidy-publish. In those situations, the likelihood of getting the industry's best editor is not very high. If that's the case, this section is intended to help you find a good editor. The rest of this book will help you better work with her or him.

Before you begin the process, ask yourself if you will be open to suggestions. If not, then don't spend the money for a full edit. You may prefer to hire a proofreader. That should cost less.

You may be able to tell what kind of an editor you're interviewing by how much he or she charges. If that is one dollar a page, expect that this may be someone who is getting started in the business or someone who will check only for grammar and spelling errors and other tracks left by gremlins. If the fee is seven to ten dollars a page, you may get not only an edit but an edit with explanations you can learn from.

The sad thing is that sometimes the fee is no indicator at all. That's why you should check the sidebar on Internet shams before you begin your search for an editor. Once you have one or two you'd like to consider, ask:

- What experience he or she has had editing works in your genre.

- If your book is fiction, will she or he give you suggestions regarding motivation, character development and other aspects of craft? This is not always essential but can certainly make a difference to your work and to your book's success.

- Can or will he or she help you with structure — things like plot points, the big gloom and denouement?

- Will he or she edit your synopsis and your book proposal?

- Does he or she supply references? (See the sidebar.)

- How does he or she charge? By the hour, the page, the job?

- What does she or he estimate the edit of your book will cost? (The editor may request a copy of your manuscript in order to give you a meaningful estimate.)

- Will the editor supply you with a list of his or her edited books and other credentials?

During this process, try to determine if your personalities mesh well.

How to Avoid Internet Shams and Scams

- Ask instructors/professors who teach in the writing department at your local university for their recommendations. Not the English department but the writing department or program.

- Ask the directors of the best writing conferences (again, preferably those associated with universities or colleges) for their suggestions.

- Beware the Web—at least, beware of finding an editor using a search engine alone. Many of the editors recommended by professionals will have their own websites, of course.

- Ask fellow published authors, preferably those whose books you have read or those published by the most trusted of publishers.

- Check the acknowledgment pages of books published by premier firms. Many use stables of freelance editors and if an author has credited the editor, he or she may be open to editing your book.

- No matter who recommends an editor, ask for references.

- Check those references. Ask pertinent questions, questions like:

1. How did you find this editor? (The answer may indicate to you whether they are cousins or best friends or in debt to one another.)

2. Why did you choose this editor over others? (If this was the only editor they looked at, that, too, may indicate too cozy a relationship.)

3. What do you consider this editor's most important credential?

4. Has this editor worked on more than one of your books?

5. What kind of book did he/she edit for you? (If this editor can't supply some credible fiction references for you and you write fiction, consider looking further.)

- Do not select an editor on the cheapest quote possible. You wouldn't do that if you were getting bids from a contractor to build a house for you, right?

Section V
The Big Galley Edit

30 ≋ The Galley Edit: Where You Come to Truly Believe in Gremlins

You wrote and edited your query letter. Someone loved your book. Yeah! You wrote and edited your manuscript and submitted it. You've worked (maybe haggled) with your editor. Perhaps you decided to self- or subsidy-publish. And now your galleys are at your door. This is your last chance to edit and, believe me, the gremlins will have done their silent work, so don't get lax now.

Diane Newton, editor of *Secrets II*, an anthology of stories about the human condition and deep, dark secrets kept or revealed, says somehow the galleys for that book didn't have "a single word in italics after page sixty-three, and . . . there are fifty places that need italics in the last three stories and just about as many in the back matter, including authors' bios and the reader contest pages." She reports that she's never before had more than eight galley changes in her life.

We not only want to avoid galley changes because anything missed in this final state will almost certainly slip into print, but also because galley changes made by the author are time-consuming, expensive and changing one error can beget another. No wonder Diane was upset. One hundred or more edits is a chore. Even when you're oh so thorough, the gremlins can getcha. It's worse, though, if you have to blame yourself instead of our tricky nemeses with the purple warts.

31 ≋ Tricks to Foil the Galley Gremlins

This is your last stand against the gremlins. You can win. Use all the skills you have learned.

- Do a first read when your galleys arrive and don't turn the corrections in. Let your corrections sit around until just before your deadline. During this down time, don't even look at the book or the correction sheet (or whatever method your publisher asks you to use).

- In the meantime, let another pair of eyes — preferably a fresh pair — do a galley check, too.

- Just before you e-mail or ship your galleys for the last (gasp!) time, read them once again. This time out loud. Poets can read lines from the bottom of each stanza to the top. Doing that slows you down. Bet you find at least one more track left by a gremlin.

If you receive a galley all marked up with symbols you don't understand, learn more about proofreading marks at this site:
www.writersservices.com/services/s_marginal_marks.htm

Journalists will know them already. Writers of all kinds will find them handy to know.

32 ⚏ Check Up on Your Formatter

I know I cautioned you about never trusting your computer. Or your publisher. Or the best, smartest, most detail-oriented editor around. T. C. McMullen (www.tcmcmullen.com), an excellent formatter, prefers clients who have faith in their formatter. Still, she agrees it is helpful to work with an author with some knowledge of the process.

Remember my friend Kathe Gogolewski? How she found that an arcane formatting rule lost some points for her when she entered a contest? Well here are some others you'll need to know more about when submitting a manuscript:

- You may be responsible for arguing with your publisher or formatter that each chapter should start about one-third of the way down the page. This space is called *sinkage* and was designed in by the publisher. That may not be true today. Your book may not have a designer; your formatter or publisher may choose to ignore this nicety because they want to save space, paper or money. If you should enter your book in a contest, a departure like this will be noticed. Can you imagine missing the Pulitzer by two points? Further, your readers will feel that the pages are cramped. T. C. says, "This white space gives readers a breather, a sort of intermission."

- Each chapter should begin on an odd-numbered page unless your text is particularly long. One of the few universal publishing rules is that odd numbers go on the right-hand pages. That may mean that a blank or nearly blank page appears in your galley. It will most often be the page opposite (on the left) from the beginning of each chapter, but blanks can legitimately occur in front and back matter, too.

- The font should never be smaller than ten-point. Twelve-point Times Roman is standard.

- Watch for widows—a single usually short last line (as of a paragraph) separated from its related text and appearing at the top of a printed page or column.

- Watch for orphans—a heading, subheading or a single line of a paragraph separated from its related text and appearing at the bottom of a printed page or column. Word may suppress widows and orphans but may, in turn, create a large, empty space at the bottom of a printed page or column.

- Check margins and other spacing. Some nonfiction requires more open space than fiction. This may be another point you'll want to negotiate with your publisher.

- Assess the placement of sidebars and/or illustrations on the page.

- Check the front matter; be adventurous here. Just know what rules you are breaking and have a good reason to do so. If you see something you don't understand or don't like, ask.

- Some publishers use two title pages. The second is called a half-title page. Old-timers may call them bastard title pages, and they traditionally appeared before the title page or any other front matter. In those days they were abbreviated versions of the title page that could be torn off before the book was bound. Your publisher may have many reasons for using two. One defense for the practice is that authors can sign and personalize one page and the book will still have an extra one that is untouched. Another is that an additional title page can separate the book's text from long and complex front matter. The setup of a book's front matter may be part of your publisher's style guidelines and be nonnegotiable.

- If your book has a contents page, just use the term *Contents*. "Table of Contents" is redundant and archaic.

- Check back matter, too. A few new ideas won't hurt, especially if yours is a book of nonfiction. Ask your publisher who is responsible for making the index. Today nonfiction authors may be responsible for them even when they are published traditionally. If the finger points at you, don't get lazy and try to avoid doing it. Anything that will help your reader is worth the time and effort. Consider hiring a professional indexer. Here's where you may find help:

  - Freelance indexers at the American Society of Indexers: www.asindexing.org/site/index.html.

  - Barbara Wallace at www.libriservices.com offers a tips e-booklet on indexing for a nominal fee.

  - My fellow Audio Divas and I have an audio that will help you do your own. In it Joyce Faulkner leads you through Word's indexing feature. The learning curve is steep but when you have negotiated the hairpin bends and potholes, you will feel confident about one more aspect of the publishing process. Find it at Double Dragon Publishing, Inc., http://double-dragon-ebooks.com/single .asp?ISBN=DDPAUDIO00002.

  - *The Chicago Manual of Style* has an exhaustive chapter on doing your own index.

- Some books include a study guide in the back matter. If your fiction could be used by teachers in the classroom or is suitable for reading groups, a study guide may be in order.

- Learn more about formatting headings and subheadings at: www.pma-online.org/scripts/shownews.cfm?id=1213. This article by Jack M. Lyon for the Independent Book Publishers

Association (PMA) provides many Word formatting procedures, including en-dashes, em-dashes and straight and curly quotation marks.

- Treat an ellipsis (three periods to connote omitted information or that an idea or speech is trailing off) as a three-letter word. This is a safe formatting approach, but because there is much disagreement about the dot dot dots, you may want to read a complete discussion on the topic at http://en.wikipedia.org/wiki/Ellipsis. It will help you even if you write in Polish—and that isn't a joke.

- Send everything included in the book to the formatter right up front unless this step is not something you can control. Adding a single page, paragraph or even a word can cause havoc for a formatter. The gremlins, of course, love it when you have to alter something after the formatting is done.

- T. C. reminds me that the programs formatters use, like PageMaker and InDesign, are very different from Word. That means a do-it-yourself approach to this aspect of publishing would be another big learning headache for self-publishers who choose not to outsource this production cost.

- Be sure your author photograph is a professional one. If your publisher accepted a snapshot taken by a family member or friend, please reconsider. Professionals do something discernibly different with the pose, the crop and the lighting.

After you've done all this, what if the gremlins win a point or two? I'll not be the first to throw stones at you or the publisher. I know who's to blame. I also know how hard you worked.

Just so you know that I do sympathize, I'm going to have a bumper sticker made. It will say, "I'd rather be writing than matching wits with gremlins."

33 ※ Heart Attacks Can Be Avoided

Self- and subsidy-publishers beware! When I received galleys for my first book, a novel, I was shocked at all the blank pages scattered throughout. This wasn't a self-published book, but if it had been, the shock would have been worse. I'd have had no one to nudge me out of my stupor. You would have been amused at my collecting the blank pages, noting the page numbers on them, trying to get a message that made sense off to my editor and losing sleep in the process. Knowing that blank pages are a natural function because all chapters begin on right-hand, odd-numbered pages (even if that means the one across from it on the left goes stitch naked) would have kept me from having a mini-heart attack.

If you publish your own book—especially if it is your virgin effort —you may run across more than one shocker. Hire help, including editors, formatters, cover design artists. Even with an expert team you'll need to have some notion of how to supervise your experts. In *The Frugal Book Promoter*, you will find a few guidelines as well as some ideas to help you partner with your publisher (or your graphic designer) on cover design.

When you hire an artist, be sure she or he is experienced in book cover design. Ask for samples and compare them with the covers done by the big publishers. These guys have been publishing a long time and (usually) are dead-center-on for producing covers that sell books.

Organizations like the Small Publishers of North America (SPAN, www.spannet.org) and the Independent Book Publishers Association (PMA), www.pma-online.org, give their members support with any publishing process they choose but are darn-near essential for those who are going it alone.

You need to have an idea about what constitutes front matter and back matter and how to order their individual parts. You need to know little facts like the one on my Amazon blog (also called AuthorsConnect™) that reminds you of the table of contents title rule I mentioned earlier. By the way, you can sign up to receive my Amazon blog by going to the page the *Frugal Book Promoter* lives on at Amazon and clicking on the button that will let you receive future blog messages in your e-mail box.

You need to know that someone other than the author usually writes a foreword, often an expert or celebrity who can lend credibility to your book. You should know how a foreword differs from a preface. Here is a site that will help you with more of the finer points of publishing: http://icnet.ic.gc.ca/publication /english/style/guide_presentation_front-prelim_e.html#preface.

You may want to download the free e-book that includes lots of helpful information on publishing at Gorham Printing: www.gorhamprinting.com.

This is only a brief rundown on formatting because this kind of information is more about publishing than editing. I included it because the more you know about this business we are in (we authors are smack-dab in the publishing business whether we like to think of it that way or not), the better equipped you will be to go it on your own or with any professional you may enlist—including those at traditional publishing houses.

Education Web-Style

If you use the Web to educate yourself, consider the credibility of the author and/or the site you are using as a reference. When in doubt, utilize the ones associated with universities. Of course, you will find recommended books for further study in this book, too. Keep reading. Check out the appendixes.

Section VI
Postal Workers Won't Return Mistakes

34 ≈ The Final Straw

You believe you've done all you can to flush out the gremlins and keep their three-toed tracks from appearing anywhere in your presentation. It's time to put your spotless letter, proposal, submission or galley into an envelope and post it.

That should be easy but even this process is rigged with traps for the unwary. My husband, author of *Everything Asians Need to Know About America, From A to Z*, once bought some extra-sturdy mailing envelopes for his manuscript because it was heavier and fatter than most (you'd be surprised how much Asians need to know about America). He dreamed that his work was spread all over the back room of a post office, papers flying everywhere. This considerate gesture, designed to avoid a similar flurry of papers, so annoyed one agent that he sent an e-mail lamenting how hard it had been to open the package (try scissors!) and how he had just tossed it into his wastebasket. So much for trying to do things right.

Another editor (perhaps more than one) hates it when an eleven-page short story is stuffed into a regular letter-size envelope. I assume that is because an envelope that looks like an over-stuffed kielbasa does not make a professional presentation. So the magic words are *clean, clear, no frills*.

I have been told by many of those who read *The Frugal Book Promoter* that a book as full of specific, practical information as this one is impossible to digest. At the end of that book (and this one!) you will find appendixes designed to help you battle gremlins by finding every entry on a particular subject. They will help you review the moment you encounter a need. They are there so that you don't need to cultivate a photographic memory. You may even find entries on subjects you forgot that I covered. Go back and reread the sections pertinent to your publishing process. Use the great online references I've given you, too. Together we can be a real force for professional submissions and a mighty challenge to gremlins everywhere.

The Mail Is Your First Foot in the Door

- Buy new envelopes that fit your manuscript. Buy several sizes if you tend to send out many different kinds of submissions.

- Use manuscript boxes when an agent or publisher requests a hardcopy.

- Include SASE (Self-Addressed Stamped Envelope) for replies, even when they aren't mentioned in the guidelines.

- If your computer skills are up to it, print professional address labels. If they aren't, use commercial address labels, print neatly, and be accurate with both name and address.

- Don't do anything cute on the envelope.

- Most of the agents who responded to my call for suggestions (see Section II) want you to follow submission guidelines and to double check to be sure all the required parts of your submission are enclosed. Do check that section for the one exception to rules that most agents post.

- Always include a cover letter. Even if it isn't required. Even if it is very short. A cover letter on professional letterhead stationery marks you as a professional. A few words in an e-mail window before you paste your submission or attach it will be appreciated.

- If you are mailing overseas and want an answer or your materials returned, enclose an IRC (International Reply Coupon) with your cover letter. Your post office personnel can help you with this process.

- Apply accurate postage. Returns for postage cost money, waste time (you could miss a deadline) and leave your envelope looking grungy. If that should happen, pop for a clean envelope.

Appendixes

Appendix One: Editing at a Glance

Of course that title is hype. "At a glance," indeed! You know by now that editing is a craft all its own. I do want to make the process as easy as possible for you, though, so here is a brief checklist:

- Organize your desktops—both the virtual and the for-real one.

- Order presentation materials so they will be waiting when editing is done. You won't want your newly edited material idling away valuable time. *The Frugal Book Promoter* will explain the necessity of beginning your branding efforts early and the review gathering process so essential to the health of your book on schedule.

- Set up your e-mail presentation including your auto-signature. See the section in this book called "Best Book Forward: Your Editing Is Branding, Too."

- Your hardcopy edits come first.

- Your computer edits—the automated ones—come next.

- Now you do more manual edits, including those done by:
  - you, including cleaning up extra spaces in your copy;
  - your detail-oriented pal;
  - your typical reader buddy;

- your final spelling and grammar checker that, remember, is only a friend when you treat it with utmost caution.
- Reconsider hiring an editor, now that you know more about this process.
- Do your galley edit.
- Check up on your formatter; she uses touchy programs and as a professional will want your extra pair of eyes.
- Check this checklist!
- Mail your manuscript to the publisher or press and celebrate!

Appendix Two: Editor's Nightmares—A Short List of Common Errors

Whether we like to admit it or not, we are living in the age of nonfiction. We are also living in an age of change. The grammar rules you knew in the sixties may have deteriorated to only guidelines. Perhaps we are also living in the age of tolerance. Or not.

Although I approve of at least one of these three premises (it may not be too hard to figure which one or ones), this book exists to keep you off the radar of those who are sticklers for grammar. We have others who define style. That means they help you decide between two right ways for doing things or between two ways for doing something where no one knows (or perhaps cares) what is right.

Mind you, it's not that people who butcher the language (or merely give it little nudges) can't be successful. It's just that most of those are not writers, they're politicians.

This is a list of a few of my pet grammar and style peeves. They annoy me because they are seen so frequently that some otherwise able writer out there will be convinced to follow where they lead.

I gleaned this list from the things I see when I read that make me stop to think about grammar and style instead of paying attention to what the writer wanted me to think about. Using my reaction as a standard is not a bad way to determine how to avoid that reaction, especially when the reader you care about may be somebody who will toss your query into the unstylish plastic container next to his desk.

These are the annoyances I find as I browse the Web, read books published without professional editors and some published with professional editors.

You'll find other aids to remedy the kinds of errors that slip by us so easily in Appendix Three. Until you can do that research, these are some of the offenders the gremlins will want you to stumble over. I've ordered them by frequency — that is, the ones that appear most often in the editing I do are listed first.

Bad, Badly. Many try so hard to get this right that they get it wrong. When you feel bad, *bad* is not an adverb. In the sentence, "I feel bad," it modifies *I* and is an adjective (known as a predicate adjective because it comes after the verb. But it's still an adjective). Unless your sense of touch has been damaged, *you feel bad.*

All right, never alright, at least in the United States. Simple as that. Don't believe me? Check www.rit.edu/~962www/grammar-misused_words.html. What if your teeny-bopper character spouts the word? You might choose the latter but is the risk of raising the dander of an editor worth it when they sound the same regardless of how they're spelled?

Quote, Quotation. When you are discussing endorsements and blurbs with agents, you may use the words *quote* and *quotation* frequently. That makes it especially important that you know how to use them. I borrowed this directly from my newsletter "Sharing with Writers":

> **Grammar Tip:** When we're writing about quotations, many of us use the words *quotation* and *quote* interchangeably. They are not interchangeable. **Quote** is a verb which means *to repeat the words of a writer or speaker*. Think of it as *to quote*. **Quotation** is a noun. It means *that which is quoted* (the words) or *the act of quoting*.

ISBN stands for International Standard Book Number. To add the word *number* or the number symbol (#) is redundant.

Awhile, A While. People often confuse the adverb *awhile* with the noun phrase *a while*. Bartleby.com says, "In many cases both forms are acceptable." The time to be super-cautious is after a pre-position. Prepositions need objects, so you'll want to use *a while* after any one of that whole list of prepositions you memorized in the fourth grade.

Only. I could write a treatise on this. However, anyone reading this book is by default a writer, so she or he knows what I would say. I will remind you that when you use *only*:

- Determine if it is needed.

- Try it out in every possible position in the sentence to be sure that it is modifying the verb or the noun you want it to.

Regardless, never *irregardless,* unless you have a character who is prone to trying to sound erudite. The snobbery gremlin is busy at other words, too:

- *Cohabitate* when *cohabit* will work, ahem . . . better.

- *Orientated* for *oriented.*

- *Preventative* for *preventive.*

- My personal least favorite is *signage*. Some dictionaries don't agree with me, but think about it. *Signage* sounds as if the word has a stuffy nose and it's so unnecessary. Plain old *signs* has functioned quite well, thank you, for centuries before somebody decided to sound more "businesslike."

Lie, Lay. If you use these verbs in anything that will be judged by others and anywhere other than dialogue, please check them out. I'm giving you a reference because I keep hearing over and over again, "I once learned [or I know] the difference, I just can't remember." I hear that even from students who learned the difference only yesterday. If you're one of those, you'll forget just as fast if I explain here. So check out correct usage at www.umt.edu/urelations/style/l.htm not more than three or four minutes before you run your Find Function on both words.

Already, All ready. Already is an adverb that means previously—it has to do with time. *All ready* is an adjective phrase; it means prepared or completely in a state of readiness. Note, there is one *l* in *already*. "I have already completed the first draft." (However, as your editor, I'd probably suggest you cut both the *already* and the *have*.)

Spitting image: This phrase is a bastardization of *spit and image*. You may prefer to use *spitting image* in dialogue or when writing narrative in your own voice.

People, Persons. *People* is the plural of person and is preferred. People seem to get self-conscious when they write cover letters, query letters and releases; their discomfort shows when they use *persons*. In *Webster's Tenth New Collegiate Dictionary*, *persons* isn't even given its own entry.

Enormity, Enormous. *Enormity* means bad, not big, at least among the literate. So says the *Chicago Manual of Style* and most other arbiters of language. You want *big*, use *big* or *enormous*.

Effete means worn out, not snobbish. Spiro Agnew famously used the word and even he probably did not expect readers to interpret it to mean snobbish—he was probably doing whatever he could to insult those "nabobs of negativity," for no one wants to be tired and he had already used other deprecatory adjectives that indicated they might be snobbish.

Myriad. You don't need the *a* and the *of* when you use the term as an adjective. It's unlikely that you'll be called on it, but plain old *myriad* will do. "Editing presents myriad challenges" is correct.

Due to, Because of. *Due to* modifies a noun, often one that is the subject of the sentence. It is generally used after some form of the verb *to be*. *Because of* modifies verbs. Here are examples:

- *The author's loss of a contract was due to her poor grammar. Due to* is part of a subject complement. Her "poor grammar" pretty much equates with "contract."

- *The author lost a contract because of her poor grammar. Because of* is part of an adverbial prepositional phrase and one would have a hard time making a case that *author* equates with *poor grammar*. Rather, the "because of" phrase answers the question why.

Since, Because. Here's one that drives me crazy. Someone on the Web saw *since* used interchangeably and liked the look or sound of it and *since* then, writers have been using it when *because* is better. *Since* is used when referring to a period of time. Use *because* when giving a reason for something.

In order to cut the crap, cut the words *in order to*. To know how to do that, study grammar help lists or *Elements of Grammar*. Here are examples:

- *Study grammar help lists in order to foil the gremlins* may be edited to read *Study grammar help lists to foil the gremlins.*

- You may also invert the clauses: *To foil the gremlins, study grammar help lists.*

Ditto for *the fact that.*

Titled, Entitled. Here's one you may fall into, especially with cover or query letters. Entitled is not the same as titled. Yep, we can use entitle to mean give a title to something but it does not refer to the title itself. In your query letters, please say something like, "My memoir is titled *Just Me*." It is incorrect to say, "I am submitting the first three chapters of my new novel entitled 'Labyrinth.'" Not only that, but it sounds forced, overly formal, labored and downright annoying.

African American, Black. In this decade, the preferred term is *black*. Use *African American* only in dialogue or if the name of an organization includes that term in its title. You may use it to describe an individual who prefers that term for herself. Hyphenate only when used as a modifier.

Literally, Figuratively. My threshold for annoyance is crossed when people slur the word *literally* and make it "litally." As I was writing this book, a publisher reminded me that *literally* is used in proposals when the writer means *figuratively.* June Casagrande, grammar guru, used this as an example for how not to do it: "They were literally glued to their seats." June, with her ever-present humor, notes that someone would have applied glue to either the chair or the posterior if that situation were, indeed, literal.

That, Which, Who. That is used for defining clauses that identify the thing being talked about. The clause it introduces gives essential meaning to the sentence. *Which* is used for non-defining clauses. In other words, you could pick up the entire clause beginning with *which*, throw it in a trash heap and the reader would still be able to understand the sentence. It gives the reader additional, nonessential information.

There are a few exceptions to these guidelines, but they should serve you well. When you run across an exception and examine it carefully, your instinct will probably let you know when to stray from the rule of thumb.

Some editors are adamant about either removing or including *that* in a relative clause when the subject of the clause is different from the word or phrase the clause refers to. Some believe you must write *the book that I was reading.* Others like to take a red pen to it so it reads *the book I was reading.* Well, I think it doesn't matter. Others think that it does. Take your choice! Generally, journalists are more inclined to deep-six the *thats.*

The time to be cautious is when *that* introduces a subordinate clause that begins with an adverbial phrase. Example:

> The gremlins find that under these circumstances they can do their worst work. If you omit *that* you can confuse the meaning.

We might expect—for a moment at least—that the gremlins are going to find something unsavory hidden under circumstances in the same way they might find a tooth under a pillow.

I like to err on the side of caution and use *that* whenever there is the slightest doubt.

What about *who*. There are those who proclaim wide and far that *who* should always be used when referring to a person rather than an object. Know that using *that* instead of *who* "is quintessential English usage, going back to the Old English period," according to *The American Heritage Book of English*. I wouldn't argue with such a respected tome, but I figure there's no reason to invite the wrath of even a few gatekeepers—primarily American ones—who swear by the *who* rule. You have too much riding on it.

Guess what. *Guess what* isn't a question, it's a command. A period after the phrase will do just fine.

Between and Other prepositions. Most of us get the pronouns we use after a preposition right. *To him, over her, on me.* It seems otherwise perfectly literate authors (like all of us) get self-conscious when writing to gatekeepers who hold our fates in their hands, but this is no time to get high falutin'. *Between* is a preposition. We say "Between you and me," not "Between you and I," even if it sounds incorrect to some. Use caution in selecting your pronoun wherever you have a compound pronoun but especially after that troublesome preposition *between*.

Try and, Try to. To keep your copy criticism free, use *try to. Try and* isn't wrong, only casual, but you won't get a chance to make your point if you tick a gatekeeper off.

Snuck. Yes, there is such a word. A very ugly one, don't you think? Dictionary.com says, "Many writers and editors have a lingering unease about the form, particularly if they recall its nonstandard origins. And sixty-seven percent of the Usage Panel disapproved of *snuck* in our 1988 survey." This isn't the time to flex your tolerance for the colloquial. Let's be cautious here—for the preservation of our reputations and to assure the success of our submissions. Avoid *snuck* unless you're writing dialogue for guys in detention at Central High. I mean, even the Simpsons prefer the more standard *sneaked*.

Splitting Infinitives. Yes, there are times when infinitives not only sound better split, they make more sense. For our purposes, however, check every verb that begins with *to*. Your mission is to weed out adverbs that come between the *to* and the verb and place them elsewhere (or get rid of them entirely). Retain an adverb with mayhem on its mind when necessary. Leave it where it is—firmly ensconced in the middle of the verb—when it makes more sense that way or when the sentence sounds funny when you move it.

Serial Commas. Many disagree on whether to put a comma after the item that comes just before the *and* (or other conjunction) in a series. Journalists and publishers of nonfiction often choose not to use them, academics almost always do. Most would agree that those who eliminate it are deviating from the traditional way of punctuating a series. I have chosen to use the AP style but I have a very good reason—I tend to use lots of asides and appositives and they require commas. I have lots of commas! Maybe enough commas to confuse. So I decided to chuck them. But for our purpose—that is, avoiding the ire of a gatekeeper—use them. One more comma can't use up that much more ink.

Numbers or Numerals. This is only for those who write books. Did you know that the style rules for using numerals (or, conversely, writing out numbers) in books differ from those in other print media? I'm going to risk extending that and say this is true for short fiction, too, but not necessarily for poetry when the poet has to consider the length of her or his lines. No, I'm not jerking you around here. Use the *Chicago Manual of Style* to learn a different set of rules for your novel from the set you use for your query letter. The ones for the novel are simpler: Any number that starts a sentence gets written out. So do all others—from one to one hundred—anywhere you happen to find them.

126

For the purposes of this book, we're going to ignore the difference between the actual words *numbers* and *numerals*; you mathematicians can hate me all you want, but the number of people (including those who write dictionaries) who know or care about the difference—if there truly is one beyond the imaginations of those who know calculus—is too few to get in an uproar over them.

Appendix Three: Recommended Reading, Listening and Help

Here are some of the people and sources I've mentioned or quoted in the text or appendixes. I've added some additional ones for readers who are finding the editing process as addictive as chewing gum.

Editing

- *Lapsing Into a Coma: A Curmudgeon's Guide to the Many Things That Can Go Wrong in Print — And How to Avoid Them,* by Bill Walsh.

- *Concordance* is a text-analyzing computer program that makes indexes and word lists, counts word frequency, compares usages of a word, analyzes keywords, finds phrases and idioms, and publishes to the Web: www.concordancesoftware.co.uk/.

- *Writing Help* is a collection of computer programs by Roger Carlson, including "Passive Word Highlighter," "Preposition Highlighter," "Adverb Highlighter," "Adverb Eliminator," "Word Frequency Counter" and "Count Lines." You need some computer expertise to set your computer's security settings to accept macros, reboot your computer so the new settings will take effect and install the programs. For more, go to: www.rogerjcarlson.com/WritingHelp/TechTips.html.

Editors

- Trudy McMurrin is an editor with decades of university press and freelance experience in fiction and nonfiction. Her authors have won many regional and national awards in fiction, nonfiction and poetry. Reach her at
  TrudyEdit@yahoo.com.
  Her blog is www.TrudyMcMurrinEdits.com.

- Barbara McNichol, editor and writer, was introduced earlier in this book. Learn more about her at
  www.barbaramcnichol.com.

- Virgil Jose, writer and freelance editor, may be reached at scribe1937@yahoo.com.

Grammar and Style

- *AP Stylebook* by Associated Press.

- *Bryson's Dictionary of Troublesome Words: A Writer's Guide to Getting It Right*, by Bill Bryson.

- *Chicago Manual of Style* by the University of Chicago Press Staff.

- *Eats, Shoots & Leaves: The Zero Tolerance Approach to Punctuation*, by Lynne Truss.

- *Far From the Madding Gerund*, by Geoffrey K. Pullum et al.

- *Garner's Modern American Usage*, by Bryan A. Garner, is complete and excellent for Americans. For our purposes—that is not to rile an agent or publisher—choose the more formal of possibilities it offers. Or, if the suggestion feels stilted, rearrange the construction of your sentence.

- *Grammar Snobs Are Big Meanies: Guide to Language for Fun & Spite*, by June Casagrande. Use this book when you want to argue with an editor, not when you want to impress one. A more formal tome that may be used the same way is *The New Fowler's Modern English Usage* (Fowler and Burchfield).

- *StyleEase for Chicago Manual of Style and Turabian's Manual for Writers* is a computer program to help you automate some of what is in this book. Go to: www.masterfreelancer.com/wsstore/styleeaseCHICAGO-download.html.

- *The American Heritage Book of English.*

- *Audio Classes for Writers,* a series of MP3 or CD-ROM lessons. The title "Flesch Readability Score: A Rarely Used Tool for Tweaking Manuscripts and Targeting Your Audience," produced, written and recorded by Allyn Evans, Joyce Faulkner, Kathe Gogolewski, Carolyn Howard-Johnson and Marilyn Peake, tackles that subject in depth. Find it at www.double-dragon-ebooks.com/audio.asp.

- *Perrin and Smith Handbook of Current English* has been around so long you might find it in a used bookstore. When you've read it, you'll know the difference between *temerity* and *timidity* – or at least know to look them up. "Half knowing a word may be more dangerous than not knowing it at all" is the kind of truth you'll find within its pages.

- *The Cambridge Grammar of the English Language.*

- *The Elements of Style, Fourth Edition*, by William Strunk Jr., E. B. White, Roger Angell.

- *The Describer's Dictionary: A Treasury of Terms & Literary Quotations*, by David Grambs.

- *When Words Collide – A Media Writer's Guide to Grammar and Style*, by Lauren Kessler and Duncan McDonald.

Websites

- A site that will help you with straitlaced, no nonsense rules of grammar: www.rit.edu/~962www/grammar-misused_words.html.

- A site that gives a lot of detail and practical tests for grammar is:
  www.grammar-monster.com/lessons/lhyphen.htm.

Craft

- *The Complete Writer* by Bev Walton-Porter, Mindy Phillips Lawrence, Pat McGrath Avery and Joyce Faulkner. Do your Amazon search on ISBN 0974565261.

- *Writing Dialogue* by Tom Chiarella is a must-read because poor dialogue technique is a glaring tip-off to editors and publishers that a manuscript is written by a beginner who has not taken the time to learn our craft.

- *Writing for Emotional Impact: Advanced Dramatic Techniques to Attract, Engage, and Fascinate the Reader from Beginning to End,* by Karl Iglesias.

Custom Dictionaries

Many professional organizations will share their print conventions with authors. Just ask. Here are a few:

- Zoologists and those who write about wildlife will find free custom dictionaries at:
  http://home.comcast.net/~wildlifebio/c_dic.htm.

- This site is for linguists and others who would like foreign language custom dictionaries:
  www.bmtmicro.com/BMTCatalog/win/msworddictionaries
  .html.

- Here is a custom dictionary for medical terms:
  www.ptcentral.com/university/medterms_zip.html.

- To find a tree and woody plant dictionary go to:
  http://shade-trees.tripod.com/tree_dic.html.

Promotion

- *Book Promotion from A to Z,* by Fran Silverman.

- *Making the Perfect Pitch: How to Catch a Literary Agent's Eye*, by Katherine Sands.

- *PromoPaks: Nearly Free Marketing for Authors*, by Janet Elaine Smith. Available only at: http://starpublish.com/starbooks.htm.

- *The Frugal Book Promoter: How to Do What Your Publisher Won't*, by Carolyn Howard-Johnson. USA Book News' Best Professional Book award and the Book Publicists of Southern California's Irwin Award winner. Helps authors build a credible package or platform necessary for selling writing to agents and publishers and for selling books once they are released.

Publishing

- *The ABC's of POD: A Beginner's Guide to Fee-Based Print-on-Demand Publishing*, by Dehanna Bailee. Those choosing to self- or subsidy-publish and thus required to do most of the detail work on their own will find this reference useful. For more information visit the author's website: http://dehanna.com.

- *The Complete Guide to Self-Publishing* by Marilyn Ross and Tom Ross.

- *The Well-Fed Writer Publishes* by Peter Bowerman.

- Gorham Printing (www.gorhamprinting.com/) has a free e-book with some helpful guidelines on publishing on their home page.

Book Proposals

- *Book Proposals That Sell, 21 Secrets to Speed Your Success*, by Terry Whalin.

- *How to Write a Book Proposal* by Michael Larsen.

Typesetting and/or Formatting

- *Books, Typography, and Microsoft Word* by Aaron Shepard. This is a downloadable e-book.
- *Stop Stealing Sheep and Find Out How Type Works* by Erik Spiekermann and E. M. Ginger.
- *The Complete Manual of Typography* by James Felici.
- For desktop publishing: http://desktoppub.about.com/cs /basic/a/textcomposition.htm.

Having Fun

- *Sun Signs for Writers* by Bev Walton-Porter.
- *The Complete Writer's Journal*, edited by Pat McGrath Avery, Joyce Faulkner and Carolyn Howard-Johnson, is a journal crammed full of quotations from old pros and newbies to amuse and inspire you.

Directories: Marketplaces for Your Work

- *International Directory of Little Magazines & Small Presses*, edited by Len Fulton, includes information that will help you target the right publisher for anything from an article to a poem.
- *Writer's Market*, published by Writer's Digest Books, has companion volumes targeted companion for markets like poetry, novels and short stories, Christian markets and more. Updated annually. Everyone uses them.
- *Writers' Journal*, a bimonthly magazine, focuses on writers who are beginners.
- *The Writer*, a monthly publication. This one seems targeted to those writing only for pleasure.
- *The Writer's Guide to Magazine Markets: Fiction*, edited by Krieger and Freedman, includes information on grants and other topics of interest to writers.

- *The Literary Press and Magazine Directory: The Only Directory for the Serious Writer of Fiction and Poetry,* edited by the Council of Literary Presses and Magazines.

- *The Poet's Marketplace,* edited by Joseph Kelly. This reference is not updated frequently, and authors need to check the facts in any targeted publication before submitting. Buy a copy of the magazine. You'll get more than current contact information from the experience.

Appendix Four: Contributing Literary Agents

I am recommending these agents because they cared enough to offer their time to make the query process better for you. Each author (and each agent) has an individual personality. Each author (and each agent) has a specific product or product range to sell. Whether you will be a match for any one of them is strictly up to you (and to them). I am not listing their e-mail addresses. That's because I want you (and they want you) to go to their websites to learn who they are, what they do and, most of all, what their guidelines are.

Laurie Abkemeier, DeFiore and Company:
www.defioreandco.com.

Jenoyne Adams, associate agent for Levine/Greenberg Literary Agency: www.levinegreenberg.com.

Megan C. Atwood, Firebrand Literary Agency:
www.firebrandliterary.com.

Jenny Bent, Trident Media Group:
www.tridentmediagroup.com/jennybent.html.

Roberta Brown, Brown Literary Agency:
www.brownliteraryagency.com.

Scott Eagan, Greyhaus Literary Agency:
www.greyhausagency.com.

Carolyn Howard-Johnson

Lisa Ekus-Saffer, Lisa Ekus Public Relations Co. LLC: www.lisaekus.com.

Elaine P. English, PLLC Literary: 4710 41st Street, NW, Suite D, Washington DC 20016.

Lilly Ghahremani, a founding member of Full Circle Literary, LLC: www.fullcircleliterary.com.

Larry Kirshbaum, LJK Literary Management: www.ljkliterary.com.

Jeff Kleinman, Folio Literary Management: 708 3rd Avenue, 16th Floor, New York, NY 10017: www.foliolit.com.

Michael Larsen, Michael Larsen–Elizabeth Pomada Literary Agents: www.larsen-pomada.com.

Tamela Hancock Murray, Hartline Literary Agency: www.hartlineliterary.com.

Kristin Nelson, Nelson Literary Agency, LLC: www.nelsonagency.com.

Gina Panettieri, Talcott Notch Literary: www.talcottnotch.net.

Stephanie Kip Rostan, Agent, Levine/Greenberg Literary Agency, Inc.: www.levinegreenberg.com.

Kae Tienstra, KT Public Relations & Literary Services: www.ktpublicrelations.com.

Liz Trupin-Pulli, Jet Literary: www.jetliterary.com.

Matt Wagner, Fresh Books Literary Agency: www.fresh-books.com. You'll find entertaining quotations from queries he has received on his blog at this site.

Michelle Wolfson, Artists and Artisans, Inc.: www.artistsandartisans.com.

Appendix Five: Sample Cover Letter

If you know or have spoken to whomever you are contacting, your cover letter may be friendly and, depending on your personal style, you may use a first name. If this is a first contact, use the person's proper title (Mr., Mrs., Ms.), but avoid stiff formality.

This letter accompanied a media kit and a reader copy (ARC) that I sent to a reviewer. As you can see, a letter that uses the Times New Roman font is appropriate. It should be single-spaced and one page only. Notice the invitation to the event at the end. When that's possible, it is both polite and smart marketing to include the press in your plans. You will find more information on what to include and avoid in chapter five—"Dangerous Corners Ahead: Covers and Queries."

Both this letter and the sample query letter are for my fiction rather than nonfiction. That is because, generally speaking, it is much easier for authors to find the right information and tone to sell and promote nonfiction. Fiction writers may need a little extra guidance.

Carolyn Howard-Johnson
Author of *This Is the Place*
Address
Phone: xxxxxx Fax: xxxxxxx. E-mail: HOJONEWS@aol.com
FREE Chapter of *This Is the Place* at carolynhowardjohnson@sendfree.com

Date

Contact's address xxxx

xxxxx

xxxxx

Dear Marilee,

It's been a while since we spoke about your reviewing my book, *This Is the Place.* As you can see, it is a bit late, but July 1st is now AmErica House's release date. Since we spoke, *This Is the Place* won Sime-Gen.com's Reviewers' Choice Award in their mainstream category. Nominations are made by reviewers nationwide.

I am a journalist who got lost for about forty years. I conceived an idea for a novel when I was writing for my high school newspaper; it gestated through my years as a staff writer at the *Salt Lake Tribune, Good Housekeeping*, my years as a publicist and for about four decades after that.

Many, including the editors at the *Los Angeles Daily News*, have found my writing a book at an age when most are considering retirement an interesting news angle. At the age of sixty-two I found a publisher, several of my short stories placed in the finals of national literary contests, I completed my first screenplay, and I started back to school to study writing.

That *This Is the Place* tells the stories of four generations of Utah women, from the 1800s to the 1950s, makes it of particular interest to history buffs and those who like women's literature. Its premise

140

is that intolerance can be corrosive even when it is cloaked in family, love and community.

As you can tell, I am excited about my novel. Its release date coincides with the burgeoning interest in Utah as the 2002 Winter Olympics approach.

I am enclosing a media kit and an unedited review copy of my novel (with a generic cover). If there is anything else I can do for you, please let me know. I have head shots, a jpeg file of my book cover and other assorted promotional materials you might need. My first official reading and signing will be at Vroman's on Thursday, July 26, at 7 p.m. and I'd love to see you there.

Thank you for your consideration.

Sincerely,

Carolyn Howard-Johnson
Encs: 2

Appendix Six: Sample Query Letters

I wish I could tell you that this query letter was successful, that *This Is the Place* had been optioned for a film, complete with vistas of the craggy Wasatch mountains in Utah. Instead, I received my book back from Mr. Redford's office. It looked as if it hadn't been opened and was accompanied by a note that appeared personal (signed by his secretary). She advised that accepting books over the transom (transom is publishing talk for material sent without an invitation or benefit of an agent) was fraught with legal problems. This new author (even one with years of experience as a publicist) had learned something new about how our litigious culture affects artists. I chose this letter for that lesson and because it illustrates that the best letters are personalized in whatever way you can find. To assure you that queries do work, other similar query letters from the same period were successful — but no movies yet.

If this query strikes you as a long shot, it is. I urge you to go against the odds. If you think your book has the right stuff, shoot for the stars. However, don't aim for stars that aren't in the same galaxy as your book. You don't have the time to waste asking people to do something that is outside their expertise or genre. I chose Mr. Redford not only because we had remote connections but because the literary quality of my books and his films seemed to be a match.

Carolyn Howard-Johnson

A query for film consideration

(Professional Letterhead)

May 28, 2003

Mr. Robert Redford
South Fork Pictures
xxxxx
xxxxxx

Dear Mr. Redford,

As a little girl, I lived next door to the VanWagenens [relatives of Redford's wife] in Provo. Later I moved to Salt Lake City to begin my writing career at the *Salt Lake Tribune*. When my husband graduated from the U [University of Utah], we moved to New York where he attended graduate school and I worked as a fashion publicist. Later, my husband worked with Richard [Mr. Redford's relative] at a consulting firm in Los Angeles. It is a small world.

I wrote a book several years ago titled *This Is the Place* because it was a story that had to be told. It has won numerous awards and I am now exploring options for a movie. Because of your interest in the West and the literary tone of your work, you are the first person I have contacted.

Set in Utah in the 1950s (about the time you and I were growing up), *This Is the Place* is a semi-biographical novel dealing with the pain and ecstasy of overcoming religious intolerance. My lead character and I are of Mormon heritage but not LDS; we're both women who tried to follow our hearts at a time when women had few choices. *This Is the Place* recounts our struggles and some of my Mormon family's pioneer stories. I overcame the effects of intolerance; my Protestant mother never did. My main character overcomes it, too. The book is a story about her journey.

144

Although I feel that my portrayal of Utah's beauty is part of its strength, a screenplay could very easily deal with Jewish vs. non-Jewish, black vs. white, Asian vs. non-Asian because intolerance is so . . . well, generic. The tone of *Bend It Like Beckham* reminded me of *This Is the Place,* and my character and I both relate to the angst Julianne Moore portrayed in the 1950s setting of *Far From Heaven.*

I've enclosed a copy of *This Is the Place* with another book of mine that was recently published titled *Harkening.* I titled the story about the VanWagenen mother (I was only about six—I don't remember her first name—you will recognize her, I'm sure) as "Neighbors" and another one set in Springville as "Summerville." You might also enjoy "Helper," a story about my father's and my adventures when he took me with him to deliver Cokes in Helper, Utah. I am enclosing copies from the review journal in which it recently appeared.

I wish you continued success and hope to hear from you.

Sincerely,

Carolyn Howard-Johnson
Encs.

Carolyn Howard-Johnson

A query with a different purpose, for a different genre

July 28, 2006

Dear Ms. Shuck,

Oriental Press in Beijing, China's largest publisher, recently published my *What Asians Need to Know About America, From A to Z*. The book's ISBN is 7-5060-2464-0. Oriental purchased the worldwide Chinese language rights twelve months into my two-year writing effort. The book has received strong endorsement, including that of the former Singapore ambassador to the UN and the US.

Not only did I write it for people in China, but for the millions of Chinese in the US who are baffled by our culture and language. There is not a one-stop source where they can learn about America, its people and culture. There is nothing else like it, but there is a serious need for it. That's why I wrote it. Reading the book is like taking a course in America 101. I distill this very broad subject into a neat, well organized, fun, and easy to understand package. Chinese-American readers will learn what they *really* need to know to help them reach their goals and lead a better life here.

The US has millions of Chinese Americans. And more than 500,000 Chinese students study here each year, each of whom would benefit from the book. Because our relations with China are expanding, increasing numbers of Chinese managers are relocating to the US, too. In short, the US market for the book is gigantic, just as it is in China.

I am helping Oriental find an importer/distributor for the US. The Book Export/Import Company in China is handling the book there. You may contact Mr. Yang at Oriental Press for more information at: songyan_yang@yahoo.com.cn.

I can send PDF files by attachment if you wish. They would include the book's introductory pages (from the English manuscript) including the Contents, as well as pictures of the book's front and back covers. If you would like me to send you a complimentary book for your review, please let me know.

Thank you for your assistance. Please let me know if you have any questions.

Best wishes,

Lance Johnson (Los Angeles)

Appendix Seven: Other Writers' Aids

The Frugal Book Promoter: How to Do What Your Publisher Won't

ISBN: 193299310X — Star Publish

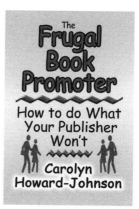

For only a few cents a day *The Frugal Book Promoter* assures your book the best possible start in life. Full of nitty-gritty how-tos for getting nearly free publicity, this book by Carolyn Howard-Johnson, an instructor for the UCLA Writers' Program, shares her professional experience as well as practical tips gleaned from the successes of her own book campaigns. She tells authors how to do what their publishers can't or won't and why authors can often do their own promotion better than a PR professional.

- USA Book News' Best Professional Book.
- Book Publicists of Southern California's Irwin Award.

Frugal is available as an e-book at the Star Publish E-book Store, www.starpublish.com/starbooks.htm, and as a paperback at www.Amazon.com and other stores, including university bookstores.

The Complete Writer's Journal

ISBN: 9780974375892 — Red Engine Press

A journal for writers, travelers, journalers and sketchers everywhere! Edited by Pat McGrath Avery, Joyce Faulkner and Carolyn Howard-Johnson, it includes more than 100 humorous and inspirational quotations from emerging and experienced writers alike.

Available from local bookstores, many university bookstores, online suppliers or at: www.redenginepress.com.

www.authorscoalitionandredenginepress.com

Authors' Coalition is a group of serious writers, both experienced and aspiring, dedicated to the support of one anothers' careers through the sharing of resources, networking and cross-promotional efforts. We provide services that augment their writing careers. The least expensive membership plan among several includes the following features:

- Subscription to "Sharing with Writers," where authors brag a bit and learn about everything from book promotion to writing craft.

- Access to exclusive support materials.

- Your favorite review posted on the AC site.

- A no-cost list of author-friendly bookstores.

- Access to the AC Speakers' Bureau.

- Access to reasonably priced AC site ads.

- Access to AC-sponsored book fair booths.

- Use of the professional AC logo.

- Access to a blog focused on making book fairs work for you.

- Posting in our AC bookstore.

- Recommendations for writers.

- Subscription to and access to featured articles (clips!) for members at *Yarnspinners and Wordweavers*.

- Subscription to *Fiction Flyer*, a newsletter that keeps writers up-to-date on the publishing industry.

Founder: Carolyn Howard-Johnson
Directors: Pat McGrath Avery and Joyce Faulkner
Website address: www.authorscoalitionandredenginepress.com

Sharing with Writers is an interactive newsletter. An entity of Authors' Coalition, it is free to all and includes tips for writing, promoting and book-related technical aid. Subscribers are encouraged to share their expertise and successes with other subscribers. Send an e-mail with "subscribe" in the subject line to HoJoNews@aol.com.

How to Make Book Fairs Successful is a blog that focuses on value-added and cross-promotion efforts. Go to:
www.AuthorsCoalition.blogspot.com.

Audio Classes. Beginning and advanced writers alike benefit from classes in writing skills, book promotion, and technology for writers. Access new audio classes in MP3 or CD-ROM at
www.double-dragon-ebooks.com/glist.php?imprint=AUDIO.

Carolyn Howard-Johnson

Learn more about the instructors and find a list of the classes at:
www.tri-studio.com/AUDIOCLASSESALL.html.

A free sample class, "Radio: A Do-It-Yourself Guide to Promoting Easy and Cheap!," is available at the Double Dragon Publishing (DDP) website. Download at:
www.double-dragon-ebooks.com/single.asp? isbn=DDP00000001QP&genre=.

Head to Head: A Writers' Audio Handbook. Allyn Evans, Joyce Faulkner, Kathe Gogolewski, and Carolyn Howard-Johnson produce audio classes for the new millennium. Published by Double Dragon Publishing. Learn more at:

www.authorscoalitionandredenginepress.com or www.tri-studio.com/AUDIOCLASSESALL.html.

The Muse Online Writers' Conference. Lea Schizas, editor of "The Muse on Writing," and Carolyn Howard-Johnson sponsor a virtual writers' conference each October. This conference lets writers— published or not—mingle with some of the publishing world's notables and attend free online workshops.
www.freewebs.com/themuseonlinewritersconference/

Sharing with Writers and Readers, a blog edited by Carolyn Howard-Johnson, is a resource for readers and writers.
www.sharingwithwriters.blogspot.com

Index

158

About the Author

Carolyn Howard-Johnson's first novel, *This Is the Place,* and *Harkening: A Collection of Stories Remembered* are both award-winners. Her fiction, nonfiction and poems appear in national magazines, anthologies and review journals. She speaks on culture, tolerance, writing and promotion and has appeared on TV and hundreds of radio stations nationwide.

Carolyn is an instructor for UCLA Extension's Writers' Program and has shared her expertise at venues like San Diego State's Writers' Conference, Dayton University's Erma Bombeck Writers' Workshop and Call to Arts! EXPO. She was recently awarded Woman of the Year in Arts and Entertainment by the California Legislature; her hometown's Character and Ethics Commission honored her work on promoting tolerance and the *Pasadena Weekly* named her to their list of "San Gabriel Valley women who make life happen" for her literary activism.

The author's nitty-gritty how-to book, *The Frugal Book Promoter* is a fine desk companion for *The Frugal Editor.* It won USA Book News' Best Professional Book 2004 and was honored with the Book Publicists of Southern California's Irwin Award. Her chapbook of poetry, *Tracings,* (Finishing Line Press) was named to the Compulsive Reader's Top 10 Best Reads and given the Military Writers Society of America's Silver Award for Excellence.

Howard-Johnson loves to travel. She studied writing at Cambridge University in England; Herzen University in St. Petersburg, Russia; and Charles University in the Czech Republic. She admits to being an English major in college but denies preferring diagramming sentences over reading a good daily newspaper.

Carolyn is the founder of Authors' Coalition and editor of the newsletter for that organization:
www.authorscoalitionandredenginepress.com.

She maintains three blogs:
www.AuthorsCoalition.blogspot.com,
www.TheNewBookReview.blogspot.com and
www.SharingwithWriters.blogspot.com.

Her websites are:
www.carolynhoward-johnson.com and
www.HowToDoItFrugally.com.